.

The New Tigers

By the same author:

The Lafayette Escadrille
High Flew the Falcons
Bold Men, Far Horizons

For younger readers:

The Commandos
Famous Firsts in Exploration
The Texas Rangers

The New Tigers

by

HERBERT MOLLOY MASON, JR.

DAVID McKAY COMPANY, INC.

New York

THE NEW TIGERS

Copyright © 1967 by Herbert Molloy Mason, Jr.

Photographs and design by the author.

Library of Congress Catalog Card Number: 67-20972

MANUFACTURED IN THE UNITED STATES OF AMERICA

VAN REES PRESS • NEW YORK

For

Second Lieutenant John Martin Luther, USAF
55th Fighter-Bomber Squadron

Who flamed out on final in a Fox Eight Four

MOSCOW, Jan. 21 (Reuters)—North Vietnamese fighter pilots train in their free time by watching birds and butterflies and studying the finer movements of embroiderers, a Soviet correspondent reported today.

The correspondent, Yevgeny Kobelev of the Soviet press agency Tass, said these "purely Vietnamese training methods" helped sharpen the pilots' eyesight and develop deftness in their fingers.

"Vietnamese pilots who have not yet had much combat experience have shown that they can fight United States aces as their equals," he said.

The New York Times
January 22, 1967

Acknowledgments

The author is deeply grateful for the unstinted assistance given him by almost countless men of the United States Air Force. Without their wholehearted and understanding cooperation this book would not have been possible. I am especially indebted to the following:

At Randolph AFB, Texas:

Lt. Gen. Sam Maddux, Jr., Commander, Air Training Command; Col. William Huntley, Chief, Office of Information, ATC; Col. Howard James; Maj. George Hennrikus; Sgt. Robert King; Maj. Paul Holter, who worked hardest and sweated blood over this project each inch of the way. Col. Woodard Davis, Jr., Commander, 3510th Flying Training Wing; Lt. Col. Frank Hammock; Lt. Col. Everett Brown; Miss Virginia Lopez; Lt. Col. William Toland, 3510th FTS; Capt. Gaillard Peck, Jr.; Maj. L. V. Patenaude; Lt. Dick McGraw; Lt. Al Taylor, 3514th FTS; D. G. Westervelt; Capt. Carey Deckard, AFR.

At Laughlin AFB, Texas:

Col. Frank M. Madsen, Jr., Commander, 3546th Pilot Training Wing; Lt. Thomas Burdin; Capt. Larry Lo Monico, Information Officer, 3646th PTW; Lt. Mike McGovern; Maj. Bradley Hosmer; Lt. John Piowaty.

At Headquarters, Tactical Air Command,
Langley AFB, Va.:

Gen. Gabriel Disosway, Commander, TAC.

At Nellis AFB, Nevada:

Brig. Gen. Ralph Taylor, Jr., Commander, Fighter
Weapons Center; Col. Vic Byers; Col. Heath Bottomly;
Lt. Col. Fred Treyz, CO, 26th Combat Crew Training
Squadron; Lt. Col. James Caldwell; Maj. George Jensen
(whose G-suit was a perfect fit); Sqdn. Ldr. Jock Heron,
RAF; Capt. Don Ware; Capt. William Meyers; Capt.
Joseph Martin, Information Officer, 4520th Combat
Support Group; Capt. Chris Wright, Fighter Weapons
School.

At Binghamton, N.Y., and New York City:

Mr. Phil Mikoda (an old friend) and Mr. William
Walker, of the General Aniline & Film Corporation, for
loan of special photographic equipment and technical
advice about Ansco emulsions.

At Northrop Norair, Hawthorne, Calif.:

Mr. Dick Hachten, Public Relations Manager, who
supplied much technical information about the T-38
Talon.

And . . .

Very special thanks, again, to Gail Peck, Al Taylor, Tom
Burdin, John Piowaty, Jock Heron, and Danny Wright
for flight experiences you simply cannot buy.

HERBERT MOLLOY MASON, JR.

Contents

Introduction

Fighter pilots are proud, clannish people. They have every right to be: even to want to *become* a fighter pilot means that a man must think a great deal of himself, and then work harder than he has ever worked before in his life in order to get the best out of himself in meeting constant challenges to his total being, challenges faced every day, whether in training or in combat. This is to take nothing away from those pilots who fly many-engined airplanes, or those incredibly gutsy men who fly unarmed light planes on Forward Air Control missions over enemy terrain, or those saviors who pilot rescue and combat choppers right into the very guns of a determined enemy. All men who fly share the same love of the air. All men who pilot military aircraft contribute equally to offensive and defensive actions that help to frustrate the Communist plan of breaking the United States economically, or bleeding us by attrition. But that fighter jocks are a special breed is something few aviators will refute.

You get to know them best in their homes and in the noisy, smoky stag bars on the base when the day's hard work is over. To have been accepted into both environments during the months when I worked on this book I take as the greatest compliment.

The Officers' Club at Nellis Air Force Base in Nevada is a splendidly furnished, gracious and tastefully decorated place. In what might be called the "back room" of the club, anytime between the hours of 1730 and 2000, you will find there a great convivial crowd of men wearing flight suits, jackets, and black jump boots. The long bar clatters with the roll of large dice poured from a leather cup; the pilots are "zapping" to see who buys the drinks for the others. You can get zapped for three or four dollars a shot doing this, but fighter pilots *always* play for high stakes, one way and another. It's worth every dime just to be able to listen to the conversation of men who have just returned from, or who are headed for, combat in Asia.

There was Lieutenant Colonel Nelson MacDonald, who flew twin-engined bombers in 1942 for the RAF. Some years ago, Mac suffered brake failure on a laden F-84G and zipped off the end of the runway, shredded his landing gear and tanks crossing "the proverbial ditch," and skidded to a stop crossways. The next thing Mac remembers is standing fifty feet away from the airplane, watching rescue men looking for the dead pilot. Somehow Mac managed to eject himself from the airplane that was dead on the ground—and lived to tell about it. He does not remember how this was accomplished. There was animated Lieutenant Colonel Chuck Klobassa, whose favorite expression is "Zing!" and who for years was a test pilot on F-102 delta-winged interceptors. And Lieutenant Colonel Jim Hughes, once badly burned in an aircraft fire. These men, whom actuarial tables would list as "middle-aged," were, in the winter of 1966, *students*. They were checking out on F-105s with the 26th Cobra Squadron at Nellis. We simply do not have enough pilots to meet our political commitments around the world, and must reach for the older hands to fill cockpits that should be filled with the younger men we were forbidden to train for the past ten years. And these field-grade officers leave a lot behind when they check in for combat duty in Thailand and in South Vietnam. In all cases they leave behind wives, and in many cases teen-age children.

Today's fighter pilot is fully aware of all aspects of the war we are engaged in with the Communists. Any of them can discuss political aims as well as aerodynamics, and all believe in what they are doing. Captain Donald Ware, 31, an instructor-pilot with the 26th, discussed at length with the author how necessary it is that we hold fast in Southeast Asia. He has been there, flew one hundred and thirty-six missions in the F-105, and stands ready to go again. We discussed the whole problem in front of a roaring fire in his home one cold Nevada night, while his son —aged eighteen months—played with the cat on the carpet and his wife prepared a first-class German meal in the kitchen. Afterwards, we said grace before the meal. Ware is not the only fighter pilot I know who blesses his food.

Fighter pilots do an extraordinary job flying incredible airplanes. But at heart they are ordinary—and very decent —men with the same hopes and desires all of us have: to keep on doing the kind of jobs we like to do, to keep home and family safe and secure. Fighter pilots have not been allowed to win the war in Vietnam—but they have kept us from losing it.

This is the story of how a man begins to learn to be a fighter jock. The process begins when he first fills out his application form and passes all of the tests. Making a fighter pilot takes years, but this is how it begins.

CHAPTER
1

HIGH
RIDE

Eleven thousand, eight hundred pounds of gleaming white airplane stand poised on the taxi strip at the entrance to runway one-three left, a wide concrete ribbon baking in the sun, stretching away through shimmering heat waves toward the barrier at the very end, eight thousand and nine hundred feet distant, and invisible.

We are waiting for tower clearance to taxi onto the active runway and launch ourselves into flight. The clamshell canopies of our T-38 are raised, giving the pilot and me the weak benefit of a hot 8-knot wind blowing from the southeast. The late morning summer sun floods the cockpit, and sweat begins to soak through the back of my flight suit, trapped in a dark spreading stain by the heavy green nylon parachute bag strapped tightly to my body. All I can see of my pilot through the canted Plexiglas windblast screen that separates our two cockpits is a quadrant of his white helmet to the left of his ejection seat. The helmet has suffered dozens of small chips. Despite the tight fit of the rubber oxygen mask against my face, harsh and unpleasant smells flow through my nostrils. The T-38 lined up on our right and a little ahead washes us with superheated gases from the twin tailpipes, and the smell of burned kerosene is very pungent. I inhale the fumes from the alcohol-based disinfectant swabbed on the inside of the mask. There is the peculiar odor of hot metal; and all of these, on a day that shows the runway temperature to be 97 degrees, combine into an acrid nauseum that makes me yearn for a closed canopy. Through padded earphones and helmet walls I hear the muted thunder of our twin turbojet engines idling at 46 percent, a mere 7600 rpm. We wait, burning fuel, for a T-38 to come in on final: the pilot has declared an emergency; every eye on the field is turned to the end of the runway, and radio traffic is nil.

He comes over the fence to our left, gear down, flaps down, nose pitched up in the correct landing attitude. But he's coming in hot and long. He flashes past at 170 knots, a white angular blur. Far down the runway his main gear scrumps against the concrete, causing tiny explosions of blue smoke. The nose pitches up still more to obtain maximum aerodynamic braking, then eases down to allow the nosewheel to bump against the runway. He rolls out of sight, down and safe.

Now my earphones come alive. Tower informs us we are clear to enter the active runway, clear for takeoff. Five or six words, two more in response, are enough. The tower input is too loud. I reach forward to the left subpanel and turn the black button marked COMM almost all the way to the left, then twist the button marked INTER to higher gain; it is the pilot's voice I want to hear, not the cryptic intonations from tower.

"Canopy down."

"Roger." My right glove moves to the lever underneath the canopy rail, flicks up the spring-loaded grip, and I pull the lever through a short arc. The clamshell drops smoothly and locks. A red oblong translucence high on the panel winks out. There is a rush of chilled air inside the cockpit as the pilot cuts in the air conditioning. The air, brought moist and warm from outside, turns to an opaque white fog. The pilot twirls a dial and the fog is replaced by a blast of hot air that raises the cabin temperature to 100 degrees Fahrenheit. Then, with everything dried out, the AC cuts in again and stays. I feel the dampness between my shoulders turn cold.

The pilot's boots come off the brakes, he nudges the right rudder pedal and we trundle smoothly to the right, to the runway, and line up, a leashed arrow. With his boots jammed hard on the brakes, Burdin, the pilot, runs through the line-up check. Nosewheel steering is disengaged. The twin throttles are advanced to MIL, military power. The master caution light is out. Engine instruments have all settled into the green. Hydraulic pressure reads well above minimum. "Let's go," Burdin says.

He comes off the brakes again and shoves the throttles forward the final two inches into MAX, into afterburner, and the engines behind my back pitch to a higher key. We begin to roll.

And how we roll! Sudden acceleration presses my back and helmet against the seat, and runway, grass, and mobile control unit whip past in a blur. At the one-thousand-foot marker we are already doing the equivalent of 115 mph. The go-no-go speed of 120 knots is reached and we are committed to takeoff. At 140 knots, back pressure on the stick is increased, the nose pitches up, and takeoff attitude is established. The needle covers 160 on the dial and we are airborne. The runway, marred by crisscrosses of black tire marks, seems to fall away. Burdin pushes the gear lever up, and the tiny wheels thump into the wells, sealed over by flush doors. Another lever is thrust upward, and the flaps glide silently from 60 percent to the full UP position. Relieved of useless drag, the Talon *moves*.

Forty seconds after gear up, we pass through 10,000 feet. I reach down and disconnect the zero lanyard from the D-ring and clip it to the thin steel stowage ring.

"Oxygen check." Lieutenant Burdin's voice is a reminder in my ears. "I have a hundred and twenty pounds of

pressure, five and a half liters and a blinker." My eyes
reach for the regulator on the right subpanel. The pale-
green eye that winks with my breathing moves up and
down in its oval lid. My system is functioning perfectly,
and I repeat the litany to Burdin.

We climb, pitched up at 25 degrees, at a steady 400
knots indicated, more than 560 mph true ground speed
at this altitude. We rush through space faster than a
revolver bullet, but there is no sensation of speed; we seem
to float in a plate-glass sky while the earth falls away
from us faster and faster. We effortlessly move past 35,000
feet, and the familiar earth is now alien, remote, lacking
in interest or significance. There is only the limitless sky
above, the glare of the sun on the canopy, the blessed
coolness of the gray cockpit, the rasping breathing (my
own) routed from the microphone in my oxygen mask,
the soothing roar of the jet engines that move us in
vibrationless flight. There comes over me a sense of such
utter tranquillity, of such pure peace of mind, that I
sigh deeply. My eyes close. I am tempted toward deep,
profound sleep.

The strange urge vanishes. I snap alert, keenly aware
that we are approaching speeds and altitudes men do not
reach every day. We move past 30,000, then 40,000 feet,
and we are still climbing effortlessly. A long moment later
Burdin eases off back pressure on the stick, and we come
over the top and level out. "Welcome to the ten-mile club,"
Burdin says.

I reach forward and stop the clock that I had set in
motion when he began our takeoff roll. The altimeter
indicates 52,000 feet, and it has taken us only four minutes
and 51 seconds to reach this other substratospheric world.

We seem suspended in the brilliant sky. There is a deep flat blue of an infinity of space above, and I peer upward through the dark visor, seeking to find the stars. They are unseen and light-years away, yet I feel closer to them and their world than to the earth which we so recently rejected.

From this great height the earth is only a wrinkled mass of brown, the color and texture of an old boot. We can see 25,000 square miles of Texas and Mexico. Sunlight glints from the surface of the muddy red Rio Grande to our right. A smear of white and green one hundred and fifty miles to the left indicates the undulating spread of San Antonio, seen along a horizon diffused by haze. A flick of aileron and rudder could have us over San Antonio within fifteen minutes, but our assigned work area is a pie-shaped wedge of sky sixty miles in radius and five miles thick. We may not depart the High Area, above 24,000 feet, without notifying ground control.

The upper air has unbelievable transparency, its cold purity unmarred by refraction. The direct rays of the fireball star which we call Sun beat down upon the canopy, suffusing the cockpit with a radiant warmth nicely counterbalanced by the AC. It is very cozy and comfortable inside a T-38 cockpit 52,000 feet above the earth, but outside the pressurized cocoon in which we travel, the sky is silently hostile, inimical to our well-being. At this lofty altitude only 12 percent of the earth's atmosphere remains; there is oxygen enough to sustain consciousness and life for a bare handful of seconds, and there is not enough pressure to keep our blood from beginning the painful process of boiling away. I hate to think of having to eject into that unfriendly crystal sky,

into the unimaginable cold of –70 degrees, a cold able
to freeze warm meat within less than a minute.

We have come out of AB and rush through the strato-
sphere in a shallow diving turn, bleeding off altitude while
picking up G and airspeed. We lose 10,000 feet and level
off with the Machmeter registering a critical .97, the area
of greatest control sensitivity of a T-38. Burdin exercises
feather touches on the controls; a movement of the stick
of one-fourth of an inch will result in going from a normal
one-G load to 2 Gs faster than you can say it. Now Burdin
e-a-s-e-s the throttles forward out of MIL into MAX. At
this speed and altitude, abrupt throttle movements almost
guarantee rpm "rollback" and possible flameout of both engines. Burdin's touch is gentle and sure. We are thumped
mildly in the back as the afterburners ignite, and the
Machmeter dial moves past the fixed white needle. Past
.97, past .98. Then I feel myself thrust forward against the
shoulder harness. *Have we lost power?* No. The tachometers indicate 100 percent. But the Mach dial has stopped
its slow rotation. Burdin explains the phenomenon of
compressibility. As we approach the supersonic threshold,
air piles up in front of the wings; it cannot move out of the
way fast enough. It is this compressibility effect that has
caused the momentary deceleration. Then we are through,
clean as a scalpel blade. We go supersonic without buffet,
burble, or tremor. The thunder of the engines is left
behind in an unseen tail of fire. We drag our sonic boom
across the face of the parched Texas floor eight miles
below, doing no damage, but probably causing wonder
to jackrabbits, ground squirrels, rattlesnakes, vinegarroons,
and other border creatures.

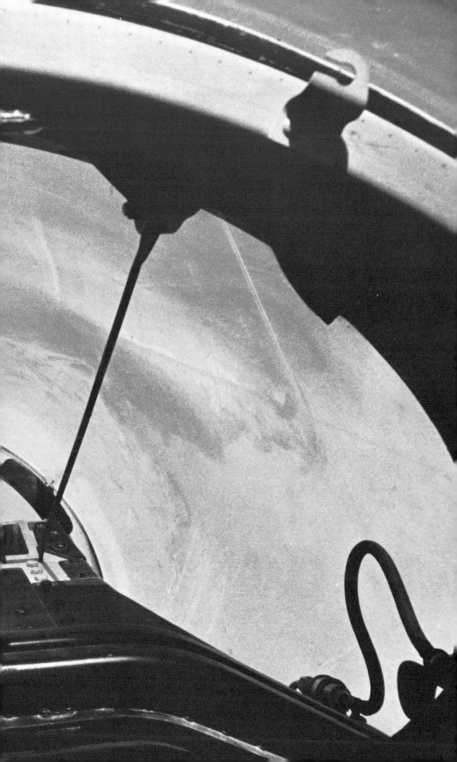

A rancher's airstrip slashes across the wrinkled face of Texas.

While still supersonic, Burdin begins to roll the sleek jet with measured increments of aileron pressure. With the long needle nose fixed on a point far away on the horizon, the wings describe precise circles around the T-38's longitudinal axis. The sky and the earth whirl in a crazy kaleidoscope of sharp color. The rolls, at Mach 1.2, are flawless. I am glued to the seat with a constant pressure; thus it seems as though it is the earth and the sky that are moving around the nose of the airplane, that we sit motionless in the air. I know better. I know that we are rolling at a rate I had not believed possible and that we are encapsulated in an alloy dart with tiny wings that is streaking through the sky at more than 800 mph. The rolling stops, the wings level, and Burdin gentles the throttles out of AB into MIL. We begin a shallow nose-down turn and slide quickly to 36,000 feet. Two miles below, moving like a comet, another T-38 races across Texas. He pulls a long contrail in his wake, but the con is sooty black, not at all like those dazzling white plumes seen from beneath.

During the next twenty minutes of flight Burdin demonstrates the fact that Northrop's Talon is truly an acrobatic airplane. Now I learn, the hard way, just why T-38 pilots zip themselves tightly into olive drab G-suits before every flight.

"Max climbing turn," Burdin warns. With the wings canted a steep 60 degrees, Burdin pulls the stick back. We howl upwards and suddenly there is the old familiar sagging of body and spirit as the G forces take hold. I am crushed into the seat, turned into a leaden useless dummy. The air bladders over my abdomen, thighs and calves come to sudden life, and I feel as though I have been girdled by pythons. With great effort I raise my eyelids and search

14

for the accelerometer. The white fat needle passes 4 and, as the turn tightens, pushes on to 5. I now weigh nearly 1000 pounds, but it feels like more. Tunnel vision, prelude to grayout, restricts the field of vision, so I can see little more than a narrow arc across the console. As G increases, the air bladders keep pace; they squeeze *hard*, keeping much of the blood from pooling in my legs from the brutal centrifugal force. We emerge from that heavy, heavy world into straight and level flight. The bladders collapse, my vision widens, and I feel like a welterweight in the seat.

"Now watch this bear," says Burdin. "No ailerons." The nose pitches up 20 degrees, Burdin eases off back pressure, and at 400 knots the T-38 begins to roll from the deft movements of the pilot's boots on the rudder pedals alone. Not as smoothly nor as fast as with ailerons, but the Talon executes stable, well-mannered rolls nevertheless. Rudder rolling is a comforting capability to know about, a capability shared in some degree by a few of the sweptwing Century fighters, but by no other trainers. Split flaps or structural damage from Vietcong flak might one day send T-38–trained pilots to the pedals to right a bird into straight and level flight to come home, to turn on final at some airstrip in Asia.

We loop, eating up 10,000 feet of sky and pulling 5 Gs. We chandelle, Immelmann, cloverleaf, and stall. We do not spin, because that means a no-recovery situation and mandatory ejection.

"Okay, you've got the airplane..." the magic words that mean I can fly this "bear." I take the stick with gloved fingertips—and wish for ballet slippers instead of the heavy jump boots Air Force pilots are required to wear. Clog-footed lunges at the rudder pedals result in sickening

yaw, and small amounts of back pressure on the stick cause large changes in attitude. The T-38 must be flown with finesse, accorded the same respect one would show a fine violin.

How beautifully she rolls! Aileron pressures are smooth and positive, but the pilot must stay well ahead of this airplane, to think out every planned maneuver far in advance. I learn this when I try to pitchout over a designated point to simulate a turn on final. I hesitate for perhaps five-tenths of a second, then enter the bank with lack of purpose—and am told I have missed the pitchout point by the length of three football fields. Chagrined, I still find it hard to realize that we are moving across 800 feet of earth during every subsonic second.

After the shortest hour of my life, while we are letting down for home, I realize what the challenge of precision military flying is about: the mating of man to machine to accomplish an assigned mission with absolute perfection. Although the ability to fly high-performance aircraft with exactitude is reward enough in itself, there is a higher satisfaction, and that is the knowledge that men are superior to even the most sophisticated machines.

But to prove this by way of putting up a pair of Air Force silver wings requires fifty-three weeks of the most idealistic kind of dedication coupled with honest sweat on a near around-the-clock basis.

The challenge is there, waiting.

CHAPTER

2

THE MISSION

The United States Air Force exists, by official justification, "in order to support national military policy." This broad statement, which could be applied with equal validity to any of the world's armed forces, acquires true meaning only when broken down into the specific missions charged to USAF's major commands:

1. To maintain general Aerospace supremacy and thus support our policy of deterring every intensity of conflict.
2. To defend the United States against Aerospace attack.
3. To conduct strategic and tactical Aerospace warfare against selected enemy targets, if deterrence fails.
4. To furnish tactical air support for ground forces.
5. To provide logistical support, including airlift, supply and re-supply of airborne operations.
6. To conduct combat support operations, such as strategic and tactical reconnaissance and meteorological studies.
7. To meet the major space requirements of the Department of Defense.
8. To provide research and development, testing and engineering of satellites, boosters, space probes and as-

sociated systems necessary to support specific NASA
projects and programs arising under basic agreements
between the Department of Defense and NASA.

With the single exception of point 2 of this doctrine,
the Air Force is vigorously engaged in meeting its every
commitment. MIDAS, SAMOS, and the highly successful
Titan III-C program see the Air Force well along toward
establishing a beachhead in true space. The prolonged
war of attrition in Vietnam has USAF heavily engaged in
fulfilling every commitment involved in a tactical war
waged against a well-equipped and determined enemy.

In late 1964, Secretary of Defense Robert S. McNamara
proved himself no prophet when he predicted that the
United States could wind up major Vietnam operations
in 1965. Six months later, however, more Americans were
committed to combat and support operations in Vietnam
than there ever were in Korea. The air war rapidly grew
in intensity until the annual rate of bomb tonnage directed
at enemy tactical and strategic targets reached 750,000
tons—more than the total amount dropped during three
years of aerial bombardment during the Korean War.

As the sortie rate rose, so did the losses. In 1965, approximately 26,000 sorties were flown against targets in
North Vietnam by the stabilized strike force of approximately three hundred fighter-bombers based in the south
and in Thailand. Operations during that year cost us 170
aircraft—more than half the number originally deployed.
Of course, the losses were made up day by day, and
planned strikes were never canceled because of shortage
of aircraft lost in combat. But there *were* shortages, especially in ordnance. Despite assurances to the public by
both the Secretary of Defense and the Secretary of the

Navy, there were periods when *no* 750-lb. general-purpose bombs were available. Moreover, combat pilots were briefed to use their 20-mm. cannon "only when deemed absolutely necessary." The country with the largest gross national product in the world, a nation that prides itself on its affluent society, was not capable of sending enough ordinary munitions to the combat zone for use by its professional pilots flying $2-million aircraft. Combat pilots were demoralized at the sight of one of the huge F4-C Phantoms "taxiing out with nothing more than a pair of Mk.81s or Mk.82s nestled among its ejector racks." The Mk.81 weighs 250 pounds, the Mk.82, 500. An F4 can carry six tons of ordnance, when it is available, which means that some missions were flown—at the risk of the lives of two men—with the airplane loaded to about ten percent of its capacity.

By the end of 1966, losses over the North, or "out-country," had risen steeply. Nearly six hundred American combat aircraft have been written off, mostly due to the intense 57-mm. and 85-mm. antiaircraft fire, but not a few airplanes have been brought down by rifle and even pistol bullets. The Russian advisers have yet to commit the MIG-17s and even more dangerous MIG-21s to all-out battle. Despite the lack of effective aerial opposition and the relative ineffectiveness of the SAMs, loss rates in the latter half of 1966 averaged one F-4, F-105, or F-101 per day. During one strike against strategic targets near Hanoi in early December, no fewer than eight USAF fighter-bombers were downed.

This kind of attrition had never been anticipated. Tactical Air Command was nearly stripped of its experienced pilots in this country in order to sustain TAC forces in

Asia. The brutal fact is, we would be unable to handle a second tactical air offensive if one were required in, say, Korea or Laos.

What had happened was simply this: years of paring appropriations for tactical aircraft and underestimating the number of new pilots needed by USAF to meet future contingencies caught up with our war-making potential at the worst possible time. True, there are enough ICBMs in silos and enough SAC bombers loaded with nukes to obliterate Russian and Chinese cities and their entire economy—but for fighting tactical wars using conventional weapons we are stretched dangerously thin. For too many years has TAC been SAC's raggedy little brother.

In 1965, the Department of Defense allowed USAF to produce only 1992 new pilots. In 1966, the figure fell to 1889. Then, realizing its miscalculation, the figure was upped to 2700 for 1967. Then, *after* the 1966 elections, DOD announced that the quota of 2700 new pilots for 1967 was being scrapped. USAF was told it could train an additional 500 pilots to help make up combat losses and other attrition. Secretary McNamara, who during 1966 was busy closing down one USAF base after another, announced that USAF would be allowed to open another Undergraduate Pilot Training Base to accommodate the new quota of student pilots. In late 1966, all eight Air Training Command bases were saturated, and it was completely beyond hope that the new increment of student pilots could have been absorbed within the existing training framework. There is just so much usable airspace in today's crowded sky, and there is a limit to the number of students even the most efficient of instructors can handle.

Pilots, once considered obsolescent hangovers from a bygone era, have never been needed as badly as they are at this moment. Manned aircraft, once written off by worshippers of little black boxes and mammoth missiles, now flail the air with thunder over a ground war fought with basically the same kind of weapons used in the past two wars. The droopy, terrifying F4-C Phantoms, the sweptwing F-105 Thunderchiefs, the older B-66 Destroyers, the F-100D Supersabres, the RF-101 Voodoos, the piston-engined A1-E Skyraiders, and the scrappy little bantams, the Northrop F-5As and the Cessna O-1E light observation planes, are flown by men utilizing stick, rudder, throttle, and instruments just as airplanes have been flown for the past half-century. Unless world Communism suddenly collapses, or American statecraft undergoes a dramatic qualitative and quantitative improvement, USAF will face a rising need for men to pilot airplanes to put bombs on target, to fly recce missions that can ferret out a single enemy soldier in a foxhole, to airlift a battalion of infantry halfway around the world, to fly in under fire to rescue a downed pilot, to pick up battlefield casualties for quick removal to a hospital, to rush ten miles into American skies to intercept and identify a bogie.

Above all, the Air Force needs men to fly airplanes because men can think through to a decision—a thing robots will never be able to do.

CHAPTER

3

THE MEN,

THE MILLS OF THE GODS

There are more American men who wish to fly military aircraft than the Air Force can possibly handle. In this, USAF suffers an embarrassment of riches: the yearly total of applications for pilot training would make a stack of paper seven feet high. Of the 20,000 applicants who qualify, at least superficially, selection boards can accept only one in four, knowing that of every one hundred students who actually begin flight training, nearly thirty will be eliminated before finishing the course. The Air Force sets high standards because low standards will not produce pilots capable of handling 1400-mph aircraft with proficiency in a combat zone, or with skill and safety in more peaceful skies.

USAF's manpower reservoir for pilot trainees is fed by five different streams. Air Force ROTC units from 180 of the nation's colleges and universities provide 45 percent of the input; Officer Training School at Lackland AFB in

Texas adds another 40 percent; the Air Force Academy's share is 10 percent, and the balance comes from rated navigators and nonflying officers already on active duty. There is no longer a cadet program; that was killed in 1961, along with the "wild" in wild blue yonder. Student pilots no longer go through pilot training as "Mister" earning $111 per month; all trainees are commissioned officers with every privilege rank can offer, including the option of being married.

Gone is the hazing of yesteryear . . . the hitting of braces, of making triple chins, the shouted emergency procedures while double-timing to the chowhall, the imagined insults showered on cropped heads by fierce upperclassmen, the double hazard of washing out due to both officer deficiencies *and* flying deficiencies. Gone, too, is most of the zest and youthful exuberance associated with the defunct cadet program; USAF does not believe that hijinks can mix with a professional approach to flying high-performance airplanes.

A married second lieutenant lives in a different world than did the cadet of what is called the "brown shoe" era. Base pay, flight pay, subsistence and quarters allowance add up to a gross $561.99 monthly. Living off base in an apartment or house of his choice, today's student commutes to flight line and classroom in his personal automobile and returns to his family at the end of the day. Before the reader jumps to any conclusions, it should be pointed out that the "commuter's" day begins before dawn, ends at sundown, and that he arrives back home utterly fatigued, facing more hours of study and longing for sleep.

All student pilots, regardless of their source of entry into the flight-training program, must meet the same irreducible minimum standards. They must be between the ages of 20½ and 26½, they must be college graduates, they must pass a Class I physical and must score a satisfactory grade on the Air Force Officer's Qualifying Test.

The AFOQT is made up of five lengthy test booklets, each designed to measure the individual's aptitude, potential, and interests. The Pilot Composite takes a measure of some of the characteristics necessary for successful completion of pilot training: mechanical experience, spatial information, and ability to interpret information received from aircraft instruments. The Navigator-Technical Composite measures ability to interpret dials and tables, to understand scientific and mathematical principles, and to comprehend mechanical and spatial concepts. The Officer Quality Composite is primarily designed to measure general learning ability and officer quality, i.e., verbal and quantitative aptitude and reasoning ability, background knowledge pertaining to world events, and a biographical inventory predictive of leadership. The Verbal Composite measures verbal skills through subtests of vocabulary, English usage, background of world events, and verbal analogies. Finally, the Quantitative Composite measures mathematical and arithmetical reasoning ability and the ability to interpret graphs and tables.

The test battery is a six-hour sweat, a brain-squeezing ordeal relieved only by lunch and coffee breaks. It would appear that only math or science majors stand a chance of scoring in the passing percentiles, but this is not so. A study of a list of one hundred men who made grades well above passing reveals that only one-quarter of the successful applicants were math-science majors; the rest had elected everything from business administration to philosophy. An orderly mind and the ability to draw the right conclusions from a given set of facts count more than does rote memory of formulae. Two hypothetical examples:

Q: *From the diagram above, if you turned crank A to the right, in which direction would gear C travel?*

Q: *Aircraft X is on a heading of 90 degrees, flying at a true airspeed of 400 knots at an altitude of 20,000 feet. Aircraft Y is on a heading of 270 degrees, flying at a true airspeed of 600 knots also at an altitude of 20,000 feet. What is their rate of closure? If the aircraft are 10 nautical miles apart at 1400 hours, and if no evasive action is taken, at what time will there be a midair collision?*

Note that such a question presupposes prior knowledge on the part of the testee that a knot is one nautical mile per hour; the rest he can figure out himself and can easily prove that the rate of closure is 1000 knots and that if no evasive action is taken there will indeed be a midair at 1400:36 hours, inasmuch as the aircraft are flying on reciprocal headings.

Imbedded in other parts of the test battery are questions probing the applicant's mental attitude, especially his motivations. Two very basic ones:

Q: *Do you like girls?*
The answer to this had better be yes.

Q: *Why do you want to fly?*

"Because my mother wants me to," would indicate questionable motivation, not to mention immaturity. "Be-

cause flying is challenging / exciting / fun," would be perfectly acceptable responses.

The AFOQT is really an attempt at printed Pentothal.
Applicants who attempt to "load" their answers are caught
out nearly every time; even the *way* in which a testee
slants his answers can be interpreted to reveal what was
meant to be kept hidden.

With the AFOQT out of the way, the would-be pilot
faces the formidable USAF Class I Flying Physical. This
can be taken, passed, or flunked within four hours. There
are fifty-five items that must be checked off on the flight
surgeon's form. The applicant is measured standing and
sitting down. He must be at least 64 inches tall, but not
taller than 76 inches. Seated, he must not measure more
than 38 inches from tailbone to top of the skull. Minimum
weight for minimum height is 113 lbs., and maximum
weight for maximum height is 216 lbs.

The dental officer ascertains that he does not have
periodontal disease and that he has a minimum of eight
serviceable teeth. A whole-mouth X-ray is taken, and if
the candidate is shown to have cavities he can opt to have
them filled by a civilian dentist and come back again for
reexamination.

The eyes, the eyes. It is in front of a black metal box
two feet long and one foot square that the Air Force loses
50 percent of its applicants for pilot training. The Bausch
& Lomb eye-test device tells all, never lies, and cannot
be outguessed. Prisms and condensers convert actual distance from eyeballs to chart to an effective twenty feet
and, again, to thirteen inches. The black sans-serif letters
are brilliantly illuminated, but how tiny they seem!

Acuity, depth perception, and accommodation tests are

followed by an examination by the testee of a black loose-leaf book filled with pages of oversize pastel dots. Hidden among the subtlety of colors are numerals that must be detected through the camouflage. Then the flight surgeon places drops of atropine in each eye. Within seconds the eye muscles begin to paralyze; the pupils open to maximum diameter, seemingly stuck wide at $f/1.4$, blurring vision. The flight surgeon peers deeply into your eyes with a lighted instrument, and you have the uncomfortable feeling he is looking directly into your soul. He is looking for refractive error, which may not exceed tolerance limits of -0.25 to $+1.75$ diopters.

You next step inside an anacoustic chamber not much larger than a telephone booth to have your hearing tested. When the heavy door slams shut, the silence is total. Ultra-sensitive earphones are adjusted until the foam-padded receivers fit snugly over both ears. You pick up an oblong of black Bakelite with a button in the center; the button is to be depressed whenever either ear picks up a tone, and is to be released when the signal disappears. You close your eyes and keep breathing shallow, waiting for a sound. The tones are unbelievably faint, shifting from lower to higher frequencies, from ear to ear. Onset and departure of the faint humming can be measured with metronomic regularity, leading the slightly deaf to believe they can outwit the machine. They wait until one tone disappears, lift their thumb from the button, then when they believe the built-in pause is over, depress the button again, anticipating the onset of the next tone which they cannot hear. But the technicians outside are on to this game and quickly shut off the signals when they see that they have a desperate man inside the booth. Test results are indelibly inscribed on a stiff white card by a stylus that traces precise hearing loss throughout the audible spectrum.

EKG, brain waves, blood pressure, blood tests, urinalysis . . . everything is measured, followed by a critical examination of the applicant's naked frame by the flight surgeon. Having endured one of the most comprehensive physicals devised by medical science, applicants sometimes wonder if the Air Force is looking for medical oddities, physical specimens without a blemish, some kind of supermen. But what the whole thing boils down to is that USAF wants normal men with normal health. The norm, however, is high.

It is a buyer's market in pilots, and USAF can afford to draw fine lines in accepting one application while turning down or holding over three others. Two factors that weigh heavily in any selection board's decision are motivation and career intent. Is the man seeking wings primarily to avoid the life of an infantryman? Does he want to learn to fly jets so that when his four-year obligation is over he can step into a fat-salaried job with one of the airlines? Such motivations have gotten men into the Air Force as student pilots, but they do not always provide the fuel needed to "hack" one of the world's toughest curricula. Obviously, USAF is seeking not only the man who has the "hands," as they say, to make a superior aviator, but also the man who intends to make the Air Force his career and who will one day be as valuable out of the cockpit as in.

And that is why the mills grind exceedingly fine.

CHAPTER
4
THE
ATTRITION MACHINE

There is no mystique connected with learning to fly an airplane, yet there are large numbers of unfortunate men who somehow lack the eye, hand, and mind coordination without which they are forever denied the right to control supersonic fighters or leviathan transports. The man who cannot pat his head and rub his stomach at the same time, the man who experiences a baffling difficulty in chewing gum while walking, are both unlikely candidates for pilot's wings. Half of the students who wash out of flight training are marked down for FD, flying deficiency.

Then there are those who discover that they are unwilling victims of chronic airsickness; every flight brings on uncontrollable nausea. A very few men discover during early flight experiences that being up in an airplane brings on an unreasoning fear of falling, of crashing, of dying; from takeoff to landing is just one long hour of fright that verges on terror. This is rare; less than 2 percent

of students who fail are so afflicted. But a surprising number of trainees exhibit what the Air Force calls "manifestation of apprehension." They are all right as passengers, but when it comes time to take over the controls and fly the airplane themselves, they freeze and tend to be-

come erratic and panicky. The "MA" students would probably do all right as navigators, observers, weapons systems specialists, but when it comes to the ultimate responsibility of actually being in charge of the airplane, they simply cannot hack it. Eighteen percent of the trainees who fall by the wayside do so for this reason. Then there are those who have no real conception of the demands flying makes upon a man: it is work, hard work, and requires unrelenting concentration while in the air and dedicated study on the ground. Sweat is a great solvent, and glamor easily dissolves in the face of repeated drenchings. After a period that sometimes lasts but a few weeks, some students begin to realize that learning to pilot airplanes is not really what they thought it was. They quit. An average of 15 percent of the washouts are thus tagged "SIE," for self-initiated elimination.

To catch as many as possible of the students in the categories just cited as early as possible and as inexpensively as possible, USAF inaugurated in the summer of 1965 a new phase of primary training. Large numbers of the reliable Cessna 172F monoplanes were purchased at an off-the-shelf price of less than $7,000 each and placed in the trainer inventory as T-41As at each of the eight Undergraduate Pilot Training bases in the country. The T-41 program is supervised by Air Force pilots, but the instructors are civilians working under contract at airports located near the UPT bases. These civilian instructors are hand-picked for the job and average fifteen in number at each of the fields. Many are former military pilots, some are hoary veterans of airline flying, while a few have as little as 500 hours in the air. Despite the disparity in backgrounds, these civilian instructors all share a common capability: they know how to teach. Students are given a maximum of thirty hours, averaging 75 minutes of air time a day during their first month in the program. During this critical four weeks the airsick, the frightened, the disillusioned, and the hopelessly uncoordinated are weeded out, leaving the basically qualified to move on to the sterner demands imposed by the turbojet T-37.

The T-41 is not an airplane to inspire trepidation, but, as students quickly discover, it is a machine that requires constant attention with hands, feet, and eyeballs in order to fly with precision.

This aluminum-skinned bird grosses 2000 lbs., spans 36 feet, 2 inches, and rests on non-retractable tricycle gear. Performance characteristics of the T-41, powered by a Continental 0300-D engine rated at 145 hp, are very respectable. She climbs at 840 feet per minute and has a top speed of 138 mph at sea level. Depending upon power settings and altitude, the T-41 has a wide cruising range. At 2500 feet at 2700 rpm, for example, a full tank—42 gallons—will take the plane 530 miles at 134 mph. At the other end of the scale, with the mixture leaned and power reduced to 2200 rpm, the T-41 will cruise for seven hours, 42 minutes—705 miles range—at an altitude of 12,500 feet. In straight and level flight with flaps up the T-41 stalls at 53 mph—and gives ample warning before doing so. It will fly off the ground after a roll of 630 feet and will roll to a stop after touchdown after only 520 feet; so emergency landings and takeoffs on unprepared surfaces pose no major problems. It is forgiving of mistakes in the air, and can absorb with impunity rough landings imposed by even the most ham-handed, clubfooted students. I have yet to talk to an instructor, USAF or civilian, who faults the T-41 in its ability to perform its assigned missions: to expose the inept, to teach the capable the fundamentals of flight.

USAF believes so strongly in the T-41 program that thirty hours were taken away from the T-37 schedule in

order that students could come to grips with the Cessna—
an airplane seen in numbers at almost any civilian airport,
an airplane surely any of us could fly.

Every weekday morning at 0700 a bus painted Air Force
blue loads up with a cargo of flight-suited men, each carry-
ing a conspicuously new brown portfolio, and heads out of
the gate leading off Laughlin AFB, eight miles east of
Del Rio, Texas. Laughlin is home to the 3646th Pilot
Training Wing, commanded by Colonel Frank M. Madsen,
Jr., from Harvey, Illinois, a B-24 pilot in the Pacific during
World War II.

The bus travels down Highway 90, turns right at "F"
Street, which bisects Del Rio, then left at the hamburger
stand on Tenth Street, and keeps going another twelve
blocks until it slows at the entrance to Del Rio International Airport, marked by a battered F-86 Sabrejet that
has flown its last, a reminder of other wars, other times.
The bus pulls up in front of a low, white wooden building
that serves as operations shack, classroom, and briefing
room for the Wing's T-41 program. The students clamber
out of the bus and march inside. The training day begins.

One of the instructors—maybe Treadaway with his
13,000 hours—presses the bulb on an oversize bicycle horn
that is mounted to the lectern, honking for attention. He
briefs on the weather and again cautions against flying
over the Rio Grande into Mexico, not three minutes' flying
time from the field. And he warns the class about flying
directly over the Amistad dam under construction ten
minutes to the north. "You fly over the thing, and sure as
hell some guy is going to look up at the pretty airplane—
and fall off the dam and bust himself. Steer clear. Now,
gentlemen, let's go fly!"

Confrontation: T-41.

Rigid adherence to
checklist obviates
Murphy's First Law:
What can go wrong, will
go wrong. Safety is ATC
watchword.

USAF teaches flying strictly by the book. There are no deviations, no lapses, no shortcuts. The process of flight begins with a meticulous interior and exterior check of the airplane, spelled out in the T-41A Flight Crew Checklist which every student keeps clipped to the zipper on the left thigh pocket of his flight suit. Pages one and two of this book list fifty separate items that must be checked off even before starting the engine. For example, the power plant section:

a. Static port: Clear
b. Engine oil quantity: Check (6 qts. minimum)
c. Engine oil cap: Secure
d. Access door: Secure
e. Nose tiedown: Remove (if installed)
f. Propeller spinner: Check
g. Propeller: Check for nicks and damage
h. Carburetor air filter: Check
i. Nosewheel tire: Check inflation, cuts or blisters
j. Nosewheel strut: Check for some extension
k. Fuel strainer valve: Check for leakage
l. Chock: Remove

Literally every square inch of the gleaming metal skin is gone over, checklist in hand, calling out the items one by one. There are special things to watch out for in Texas. You remove the canvas cover on the Pitot tube and stand on tiptoe to peer inside the one-eighth-inch opening; border spiders are fond of spinning webs in the dark, narrow recess of the Pitot and sometimes have to be reamed out with a pipe cleaner. I once reached down to

remove the wooden chock on the nosewheel, but was
stopped by my IP (instructor-pilot) First Lieutenant John
Piowaty, who suggested I use my boot to kick it away.
"We've had some nasty surprises down here in Texas.
Scorpions, vinegarroons . . ."

When the ship is untied, unchocked, and inspected, it
is ready to be mounted. The student gets into the left seat,
the instructor sits by his side at the right. You rack the
seat forward, cinch the seat belt, and stow your hat.
Attitude and heading indicators are caged and the altimeter set to field elevation. You set the clock, adjust the
cockpit air vents, and release the parking brake. You move
the wheel and the rudder pedals through their full amount
of travel, visually checking aileron, rudder, and elevator
movement. Then the parking brake is set again, and you
are now ready to start the engine.

The fuel mixture lever is set to rich, and the throttle is
cracked a quarter-inch. You set the carb heat to cold and
flick on the master switch. You work the primer until
you can hear the fuel squishing, then stick your head
partway out of the hinged window and yell "Clear!" before
turning the ignition switch to ON. The Continental explodes into life, and the two-bladed propeller becomes a
silvery blur. The throttle knob is eased back until the
needle on the tachometer slides around the 1100 rpm.
You hold it there until the oil pressure gauge gives a
satisfactory indication—within thirty seconds or you abort
the flight. When the generator warning light goes out you
turn the radio on, check the airspeed indicator, vertical
velocity (rate of climb) indicator and suction gauge and
release parking brake. Now the Cessna is ready to roll.

To taxi from the parking ramp to the runway requires a great deal of care, and the first time students try it they are hit hard with the realization that controlling an airplane, even on the ground, is indeed *not* like driving a car. Taxiing at normal speeds, i.e., no faster than a brisk walk, ailerons and rudder have almost no effect on maneuverability. Rudder pedals control nosewheel steering only 10 degrees on either side of center; after that you've got to get on the brakes to gain a maximum deflection of 30 degrees left or right of center. Torque induced by the rotation of the prop has a tendency to yaw the plane to the left, so you give it a little right rudder, just in case, and stab at the right brake to correct. But too hard! Perversely, the airplane obeys your command and pulls to the right, too far to the right. You come off the yellow centerline stripe headed for the verge. You stab at the left brake, too late and too hard. The plane slews counterclockwise and barges across the stripe from another direction. "I've got the airplane," the instructor says, and an instant later the Cessna is obediently rolling dead center. "Try it again," he says. "Gently. And stay ahead of the airplane."

The Cessna is somehow brought safely past the other airplanes, down the taxiway between the hangars, turned sharply left down an inclined ramp to the main runway, and lined up in echelon behind four others who are waiting for takeoff. You are bathed in sweat, and it is not only from the summer sun beating down on the metal top and sides of the cockpit. The others go off into the air; then it's your turn. You complete the engine run-up check —1600 rpm, engine instruments in the green; ignition system, right, then both; left, then both; carb heat (hot, then check for rpm drop, then cold) and back off on the throttle to 1100 rpm. Check flight controls for freedom of movement, uncage the gyros, rotating beacon to ON, flaps UP, cabin doors and window closed, and check the time.

Check, check, and check again; ninety-two checks before that moment of brake release for takeoff roll. Why? To avoid accidents such as the one that killed a civilian pilot in a Cessna 172, a civilian who apparently believed that checks were for chickens. His wheels left the runway and he established a good climb attitude; but at 100 feet he discovered that the control column was stuck, as though imbedded in concrete. He pulled off power; the plane stalled in a nose-high attitude, fell off on one wing, and plunged back to the ground. A post mortem on the airframe revealed that some careless ground crewman had not bothered to secure the controls with the standard locking pin—such being not readily at hand—but with a two-inch bolt. The pilot's failure to check full travel of the controls before takeoff cost him his life.

Now, there is no more to check; there is only the takeoff roll to execute, and to fly.

You come off the brakes and pull the throttle open. The T-41 moves down the runway, kept straight by gentle application of rudder. When the indicated airspeed reaches 60 mph, the airstream flowing over the control surfaces makes them fully responsive; a touch of back pressure on the wheel and the nose lifts enough to raise the nosewheel off the runway. All you must do now is keep the wings level with small inputs of aileron, remembering torque and the necessity of giving this Cessna measured amounts of right rudder—and right rudder is the T-41's handmaiden of good flying under any high-power, low-airspeed maneuvers. Before the needle hits 70 mph IAS the main gear comes off the runway and you are flying; the chain of gravity that has held you earth's prisoner has been severed.

Airspeed builds rapidly to 90 mph. Increased pressure on the elevators is fed back to the control column, requiring conscious effort to hold the wheel back. You reach down with your right hand, find the trim wheel and rotate it slowly until the back pressure is relieved and the wheel rests easily in your left hand. You quickly learn that flying the T-41 is a one-handed operation; the right hand is kept busy flying from throttle to trim wheel in order to maintain the desired flight attitudes and speeds, leaving the left hand by itself on the wheel.

At 500 feet you exit from the traffic pattern in a shallow turn to the right of 45 degrees, toward the Rio Grande. You fly this leg for twenty seconds, then turn again to the right, paralleling the river and on a reciprocal course. Down there, to the right, you can see the runway you just left. T-41s are still lining up and taking off. They seem small, no larger than silver mosquitoes. The field drifts backwards. You keep climbing, constantly switching your attention from airspeed and vertical velocity indicators and the attitude indicator to the wingtips and some reference point on the windshield that bisects the horizon. Composite flying, it's called: cross-checking flight instruments against outside visual reference points. You climb to 4000 feet and level off. You come back on the power until the IAS is 110, then reach for the trim wheel and trim the aircraft for level flight. Ahead stretches a seem-

ingly endless dun-colored swath of Texas, a hundred or
so square miles of which will become important to you
as a pilot because of the ground references it affords: the
dam, a curve of the muddy river, a ranch house, the cross-
roads, barbed wire fences, windmills, black holes in the
earth that are entrances to unexplored caverns ... even
individual salt licks and feeding troughs for goats and
cattle.

But above there is only the sun in a bright blue sky; a
new world for the taking.

That first heady flight that proves to the student that
he can indeed control a ton of aerodynamic machinery
through the fluid medium of air occasionally builds false
confidence, and it is usually during Contact Lesson Three
that this ego-balloon is popped. The third hour of dual,
known in the syllabus as C 3, painfully exposes lack of
coordination that is partially inherent, partially developed
through experience. It goes like this:

After takeoff and climbout to 4000 feet the instructor
calls for a precision turn of 90 degrees. On a heading of
270, this means the rollout and resumption of straight and
level flight should find the aircraft on a heading of 0
degrees, i.e., due north. The student clears the area to
his right, applies right aileron and a touch of right rudder
and keeps his eye glued to the heading indicator. He is
pleased with himself because he remembers that he is
going to have to anticipate the indicator and begin the
rollout several degrees before the needle on the indicator
swings in its alcohol bath to 0. He rolls out smartly, the
wing comes up level, and the plane is off course by only
half a degree. The instructor says that the turn was all

right, but that he forgot to take note of either the vertical velocity indicator or the IAS and that during the turn he maintained a nose-down attitude which cost them 150 feet of altitude. Why? Because the student failed to remember that during a medium turn of 40-degree bank you must add back pressure to maintain a constant pitch attitude due to loss of lift that always occurs when the wings are banked. On the next attempt the student, who feels "burned" at his stupidity, may become fascinated with the vertical velocity indicator, ensuring that he is not losing altitude in the turn, meanwhile not keeping track of the heading indicator, with the result that he fails to anticipate the rollout and comes up level 10 degrees off the mark. The warning is clear: fixation on one instrument can bring a pilot to grief.

The student progresses from 90-degree turns to 180s, 270s and then to 360s—a complete circle in the sky that, if properly executed, will find the aircraft on the same heading and with the same altitude with which he started. All during his student career he will be executing clearing turns before every maximum performance maneuver, and he gets plenty of practice during the T-41 phase. Clearing turns are simply two precision 90-degree level turns, one executed immediately after the other, and preferably in opposite directions. One to the right, then one to the left will bring the aircraft back to the same heading and serves the purpose of clearing the sky around you so that the possibility of a midair collision is lessened.

Next the student becomes intimate with the behavior of the airplane when it is deliberately mishandled. Mixture is set to rich, carb heat to cold, the throttle is set at low cruise, and the gyros are caged. Two clearing turns are done, then the control column is honked back until the nose is pitched up at 40 degrees. The aircraft climbs, but not for long. Speed sags, you've got to get on the rudder to keep the ship from yawing, and then, just before the shudder runs through the length of the ship, the stall warning horn begins its raucous buzzing. Then, the wings robbed of all lift, the Cessna stalls. Back pressure is released, the nose drops, and you keep your boot on the right rudder. She comes out of it nicely when you ease back on the wheel as airspeed increases. Haste in recovery, the instructor points out, will only lead to a secondary stall arising out of partial recovery from the first.

In C 3, as with most units in the training program, one step leads directly to another. Stall instruction is followed by learning the process of a power letdown, which leads the student into other exercises and, usually, into difficulty. Power letdowns are practiced so that students can ease the airplane down from altitude into the traffic pattern at cruise airspeed. Drop the nose and begin a turn while pulling off power to maintain a rate of descent of 500 feet per minute at an IAS of from 110 to 130 mph. Gentle turns are executed throughout the descent, and the wings are brought level and the nose pitched up 100 feet before reaching the desired altitude. Leveled off at 800 feet, the instructor demonstrates with ridiculous ease what is known as a "coordination exercise."

He smoothly whips the airplane into a continuous series of turns from left to right and back again. The Cessna traces a sinuous path through the sky like a disciplined cobra, 40 degrees on either side of a point fixed on the distant horizon. It appears simple, but as the student discovers, the maneuver requires the utmost in coordination of hands, feet, eyeballs, and mind. Rudder and aileron pressures must be blended in the right proportions to avoid slipping or skidding. As the angle of bank increases, back pressure on the control column must be added in precise amounts to avoid gaining or losing altitude; then this same pressure must be eased off as the wings come level and lift is regained—then re-applied in inverse amount as the airplane rolls into opposite bank. It is a continuous process in which hands and feet are moving in concert and in opposing directions, complicated by the absolute necessity to clear the surrounding area of sky before entering each turn *and* keeping always in sight the reference points chosen as rollout points. It isn't good enough to come close to these points, to maintain approximate altitudes; USAF means by precision flying, in this case, losing or gaining no altitude and rolling out *on* the points.

The final two exercises in C 3 involve flying a rectangular course and making S-turns across a road. From 800 feet a rectangular field, or a patch of ground bordered by roads, is chosen and the student is directed to fly the airplane so that it follows the ground track. Entry is made on the downwind leg, which means the student must allow for tailwind and make his turn sooner than if he were flying in a no-wind condition or against the wind. He must allow for crosswind effects at the opposite sides of the rectangle, i.e., turning more than 90 degrees into the crosswind on the downwind leg, and less than 90 degrees on the upwind leg. He must learn to crab into the wind in order to make a straight-line track along the

Pre-briefing, dual sortie, then the magic moment when IP turns student and airplane loose for unforgettable first solo flight.

ground reference line. To fly a good rectangular course requires perfect timing and a feel of what the airplane is doing every second of flight.

S-turns across a road are almost always done with the wind blowing 90 degrees or thereabouts to the road. The idea is to describe a giant S so that the ground track describes semicircles of equal size on either side of the road. This maneuver requires knowledge of when to make shallow banks (upwind) and when to initiate medium banks (downwind). And again there is the constant meshing of rudder, aileron, elevator, and eyeballs in order to describe perfect semicircles with and against a sometimes capricious wind.

Unit C 3 leaves no doubt in any student's mind that to fly with precision means hard work and the ability to think always seconds ahead of the airplane. It gives him a clear knowledge of the element through which he flies, and it sharply points up his own shortcomings and demonstrates how very much there is to learn to stay ahead of the game.

After every flight, student and instructor sit facing each other across a table, and the student listens while the instructor goes over the entire seventy-five minutes. The student watches while the older hand fills out the daily report sheet, grading each step from "Unable" all the way to "Excellent"—but the latter mark is seldom given. The student is told, at length, where he is having trouble and why and how to correct. The student has a clear idea at all times how he is making out, whether he stands a good chance of making a pilot or not. There are no surprises.

The T-41 phase is split in two parts—thirty hours for

those student officers who were not trained under the Flight Instruction Program, if they graduated from ROTC, and eighteen hours for those who were. The FIP student already has obtained his civilian pilot's license when he enters USAF flying training, a license earned while still in college. Does this make him a better pilot than his brothers who come into USAF flight training cold? Not necessarily. Numbers of T-41 students complain that at their particular ROTC unit flight instruction, although reasonably competent, was geared to civilian attitudes and bore little relation to demands and procedures imposed by the Air Force at UPT bases. Thus some students not only have to unlearn sloppy flying habits already taught them, but must suddenly reorient their attitudes toward completing lengthy, painstaking checklists. One FIP graduate had his name on the "goof board" at Del Rio International for rushing his preflight. He tried to taxi off the parking ramp while still chained to several tons of concrete. This cost him five points and a nickel to the goof fund, plus a large amount of chagrin.

Air Force pilots perform mid-phase and final checks on all T-41 students who get that far. The mid-phase comes between fifteen and seventeen hours of flying time, usually after the student has logged six or eight hours of solo. The final check is done between twenty-three and twenty-seven hours of total flying time, and this is the one that counts more than any other. The student must skillfully execute chandelles, lazy eights, maximum-performance climbing turns, recovery from stalls, simulated forced landings, ground track maneuvers, traffic pattern stalls, accuracy landings, and whatever else the IP requests. No student is downgraded to the point of elimination because of inability to perform any one maneuver; pink slips are issued for overall poor performance.

Interestingly enough, students queried who were ending the training program—men with a hundred or so hours in the supersonic T-38—almost universally agreed that the toughest part of the whole fifty-three-week curriculum is the first four weeks.

"You learn to fly that little Cessna," one said, "and you feel you've got the whole thing made."

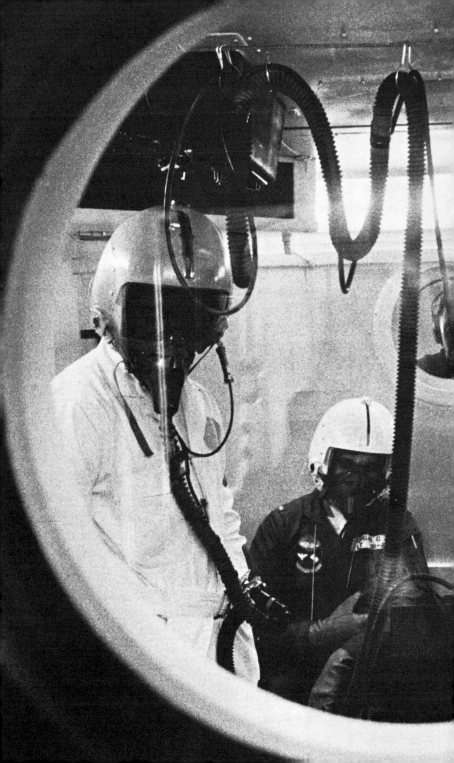

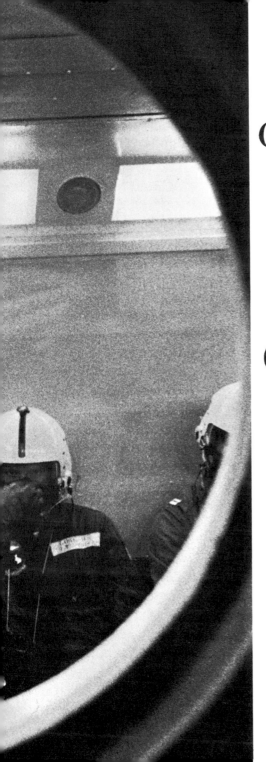

CHAPTER 5

THE CRUEL SKY

Student pilots are often dismayed to discover that the body which they so confidently move about on earth can fail them disastrously when taken aloft, away from the comforting pressure world found at sea level. The atmosphere, unseen, unfelt, unnoticed, is so taken for granted that it is difficult to realize that a column of air above only one square foot of the earth's surface weighs nearly a ton. But a few minutes straight up, as the jet flies, this life-sustaining envelope is cruelly thin, totally useless to the well-being of man. As pilots, students will spend thousands of hours of their professional lives in a hostile world; they are prepared for survival in that world by an intensive forty-two hours of physiological training, 95 percent of which is given within the first thirty days of flight training, long before the problem of survival at altitude can become acute. Students emerge from classrooms and from the altitude chamber with a clear understanding of why man out of his environment is a wretched creature, prey to a host of crippling and even killing maladies. More important, they learn how intelligent use of their support equipment can keep them alive and functioning five and ten miles above the earth.

Current physiological indoctrination begins early, starts with basics, and goes deep. Using stand-up lecturers equipped with 16mm color sound films, 35mm slide presentations, charts, chalk-and-greenboard talks and programmed texts, ATC's Physiological Training Units begin hitting students hard on the eighth day of the fifty-three-week course with detailed studies of subjects such as Physics of the Atmosphere, Respiration and Circulation, Decompression Sickness, Hypoxia, Physiological Effects of Speed and Acceleration, Sensory Illusions and Spatial Disorientation, Oxygen Equipment . . . and several others, all having to do with the crucial problem of staying alive while in flight during potentially dangerous situations. Through costly experience, USAF has learned that ignorance kills. During World War II, 110 aircrewmen died from oxygen lack in the skies over Europe, and an additional 10,000 reached the point of unconsciousness for the same reason and had to be revived by buddies, often in the middle of combat. Major George F. Hennrikus, who flew twenty-five missions in B-17s over Germany, recalls that his indoctrination to altitude as a cadet in 1943 consisted of "one or two short lectures and a brief chamber ride, where I suffered acute pain in my right wrist from the bends. I knew that oxygen was sort of important when you flew above 10,000 feet, but had only the vaguest idea of what caused the bends or how you could make the pain go away."

Perfection of pressurized cockpits in jets that hauled pilots eight miles high provided near living-room comfort, and improvements in oxygen-supply systems all but obviated the danger of hypoxia. But pilots of the last decade had such sublime faith in their equipment that many felt they could afford to be careless. What this attitude can lead to is shown by what happened some years after the Korean War.

Two F-86 jet fighters, scheduled for a routine gunnery mission over Nevada, lifted from the runway in tight formation. The wingman had a clear view into the cockpit of the lead aircraft, which was only ten feet away. As the sweptwing interceptors boomed for altitude the wingman noted that his element leader had unfastened his oxygen mask, letting it dangle from one strap on his helmet. The wingman watched as the other pilot slipped a package of cigarettes from his flight suit pocket, took one out, placed it in his mouth and casually lit up as though he were sitting in the lobby of some fine hotel. The air conditioner would take care of the exhaled smoke, but still . . .

When the planes leveled off at 17,000 feet, the wingman observed that the element leader had snubbed the first cigarette and was lighting another. What the chain-smoker did not know was that his canopy seal had developed a leak and that the cabin pressurization had seeped away; he was breathing the thin air found at 17,000 feet, his life-sustaining mask hanging useless near his cheek. Before they reached the gunnery area the lead F-86 began to weave drunken patterns in the air. Alarmed, the wingman tried to reach the leader on the UHF radio, but received no response. A moment later the F-86 pitched up wildly, hit a high-speed stall, and whipped into an inverted spin. The wingman, following in a wide spiral, was still screaming futilely into his mike when the F-86 crashed on the desert floor.

Autopsy indicated that the pilot was probably unaware that he was even in trouble, that he was unconscious when he crashed. Analysis revealed a 50-percent saturation of his blood with carbon monoxide, all inhaled from two cigarettes while disconnected from the oxygen supply that could have saved his life.

The causes and effects of the killer, hypoxia, are gone into with careful attention to detail by Physiological Training Unit instructors, many of whom have Master's degrees in one of the bio-sciences. Following is an extract from one of the class lectures given to all UPT students.

"The function of breathing is to get oxygen into the

bloodstream and to get the carbon dioxide out. This exchange is made in the lungs through several million tiny sacs and blood vessels. These sacs have a total surface area of between 700 and 800 square feet—that's forty or fifty times the skin surface of the entire body. These sacs are only 1/50,000 of an inch thick, and they are moist and porous, which allows the air to be pushed through, and through the small blood vessels surrounding each sac. These vessels are connected with a large artery carrying blood from the heart to the lungs, and with veins carrying blood back to the heart.

"The red cells in the blood pick up oxygen as they pass the lungs, and at sea level they really saturate themselves with oxygen—up to 95 percent of their total capacity. This oxygen is distributed throughout the body and is easily released into the body tissues, which are under low pressure. When the oxygen is released, the waste carbon dioxide is picked up, carted back to the lungs, and dumped when you exhale. That's the cycle that feeds your body and your brain every nine to fourteen seconds at sea level, where the atmospheric pressure is 14.7 pounds per square inch. Upstairs, it's something else again.

"At 18,000 feet, for example, atmospheric pressure drops in half, to 7.34 psi. And so, of course, does the pressure of oxygen itself—to 1.5 psi, and that is *not* enough to saturate the red cells. Saturation drops to only 70 percent. Brain tissues, which have the highest oxygen requirement, are the first to strangle. Breathing ambient air at that altitude will have a pilot dizzy and uncoordinated within five minutes, and a few minutes after that, the lights begin to dim, and you face unconsciousness."

Instructors go on to explain that hypoxia's worst trait

is its stealth. Its onset is insidious. The warnings are vague, even pleasant, and strike different pilots in different ways. Some men undergo striking personality changes, which they are unaware of. A pilot may become euphoric; he feels as though he has just had two shots of 100-proof bourbon; he may feel like bursting into song. Others become nettlesome, prone to shout abuse at others in the formation or at mobile control for imagined wrongs. Sleepiness, headaches, vision impairment, lack of muscular coordination, cyanosis—that blueing of the skin under the fingernails caused by reduced hemoglobin in the capillaries—all are symptoms of hypoxia, none of which a pilot can afford to disregard, under pain of sudden extinction.

With every breath we take, the body absorbs a mixture of 78 percent nitrogen and 21 percent oxygen. This nitrogen that is absorbed into body tissues is kept there so long as the atmospheric pressure remains normal. But an unprotected human being jerked suddenly to an altitude of 30,000 feet or more faces the danger of the bends, a malady usually associated with deep-sea divers. At an altitude of six miles, atmospheric pressure drops to 3.46 psi, allowing the nitrogen to come out of solution in the tissues, forming bubbles in arm or leg joints. The higher the altitude, the longer the stay, the worse the pain. The effect of bends has been described by one pilot as "like having tiny slivers of sharp rock packed in the joints. The pain is excruciating." Older, fatter pilots are more susceptible to this crippling form of decompression sickness than any others.

Going on 100-percent oxygen prior to flight will result in denitrogenization of the tissues, thus obviating the danger of an attack of the bends. Some pilots, however, occasionally suffer side effects of prolonged breathing of pure oxygen. They may be stricken with the chokes, a stabbing chest pain combined with a fit of dry, painful coughing that can eventually lead to blackout.

Paresthesia, known to pilots as the "creeps," is another form of the bends that is more annoying than crippling. Evolved gas bubbles reach just below the surface of the skin, providing steady stimulus to the many different kinds of subcutaneous nerve receptors. The resulting sensations make the pilot feel as though hordes of small ants are running loose underneath his flight suit, and the maddening itching can only be relieved by descending to lower altitude where increased pressure will force the bubbles back into solution.

Although few pilots actually suffer from these low-pressure dysbarisms—they are protected by pressurized cockpits, modernized oxygen systems, and partial-pressure suits—no pilot can avoid running afoul of Boyle's Law. The average man has thirty feet of intestines containing an average of one quart of gas. The law states that gas expands in proportion to lowering of pressure. At 16,000 feet, one quart of gas becomes two; at 39,000 feet, one quart becomes seven, and at 50,000 feet it balloons to 4¼ gallons. Obviously this expanded gas must be valved off in stages, or else acute discomfort will turn into real pain.

Captain Larry G. Hodge, who runs the altitude chamber at Randolph AFB, cautions his refresher trainees against false modesty. "There was this student," Hodge recalls, "who was taking his first indoctrination to altitude, and I noticed that he was looking strained when we passed through 20,000 feet. He assured me he was all right, so

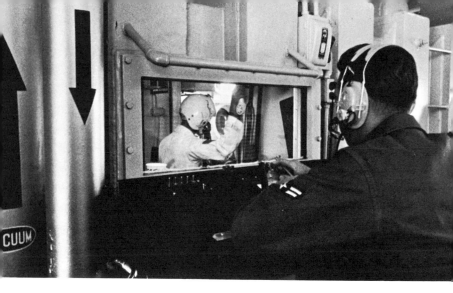

Decompression chamber, where men meet silent enemies at high altitudes without ever leaving the ground.

Two minutes without oxygen produced this scrawl.

we went on up to 40,000, and the guy keeled over suddenly, out cold. We repressurized the chamber, and the kid came to mumbling, 'All that gas. The pain . . . it was killing me.'

"I asked him why he didn't belch or pass it, and he sheepishly admitted that his mother had stressed the fact that gentlemen didn't *do* such things." Hodge convinced the student that what may be considered a social blunder in one environment becomes a necessity of survival in another.

The standard USAF altitude chamber seen from outside resembles a squat, massive bank vault with thick glass windows. Inside, the austere white walls, the flat, harsh lighting, the bench seats, the total lack of creature comforts combine to produce the uneasy feeling that you have entered a place of execution—a feeling that is heightened when the heavy steel door thuds shut against the rubber gasket, sealing you inside this monolith of steel and iron.

Twenty men, sitting beside black metal oxygen consoles, begin the flight that never leaves the ground by sitting quietly, breathing 100-percent oxygen at sea-level pressure. This quarter-hour of measured breathing does not pass in silence; there is continual chatter from the instructor outside, whose easy, confident tone is calculated to put men at ease. He reviews the facts of flight physiology, preparing us for the bodily reactions that lie ahead. He reminds us that pain that a man can bear at sea level becomes insufferable at 30,000 feet and that a chamber flight is no time to show courage in case of malaise.

The first jump is to 5,000 feet, where there is considerable pressure differential. As the great pump begins to suck the air from the chamber we yawn and swallow to clear the passages. Eardrums pop, not painfully, as the pressure is equalized. We drop back to sea level accompanied by an inrush of cold air whooshing through the ducts underneath our feet. The giant pumps start up again, and we climb to 10,000, then to 30,000, past the bends threshold. We jump to a chamber altitude of 43,000 feet and experience for the first time breathing under pressure. At that altitude there is not enough pressure to feed oxygen into the lungs; it must be forced there. The normal breathing process is reversed. Oxygen under pressure is pushed down our throats, then spat out into the exhalation valves in our masks. The procedure is awkward at first, but with practice becomes automatic.

On command, we jerk the little round wooden knob known as the "green apple" that activates the emergency bailout bottle, and we breathe from that. We are simulating a free fall—as in a parachute jump—from 43,000 to 25,000 feet. *Whumph!* The chamber fills with cold white fog as pressure increases. We fall 18,000 feet within less than sixty seconds. No sweat.

We stay at a pressure altitude of 25,000 feet for the most significant phase of any chamber flight: actual demonstration of hypoxic hypoxia. Upon command, we even-numbered men unfasten our masks and let them dangle. The others, still attached to their rubber snouts, turn to watch.

I am handed a spiral pad and told to write whatever comes to mind. I choose a familiar serial number, 567196, and begin to etch the numbers neatly on the ruled lines. One minute passes, then two. I glance at the men on the opposite side of the chamber; they are only eight feet away, but their images are blurred. I look back at the series of numbers on the page; they are still in sequence but look progressively more ragged, like a child's scrawl. I look at my fingernails, which are a sickly blue from the quick outwards. A voice breaks through the worsening mental fog. "How do you feel, Number Ten?" I give him the thumbs-up sign and keep scribbling.

"Observe Number Ten," the controller on the outside says. I look around, then realize he is talking about me. "He's hyperventilating. Notice how fast he's breathing, and how deep." Overbreathing can knock a man out almost as fast as underbreathing. To compensate for the lack of air at 25,000 feet I had stepped up the rate to thirty-two times a minute—twice that normally required. Carbon dioxide was being eliminated far too rapidly, and it's the amount of CO_2 in your bloodstream that controls breathing rate. Now I began to get dizzy. My toes and fingers were numb. White spots danced in front of my eyes. "Ten, you've been off oxygen nearly four minutes. Hook up." I did, and felt much better after a few draughts of that wonderfully thick oxygen pumping faithfully inside my mask. I watched, fascinated, as the blue color began to retreat from the tips of my fingernails.

The odds were next, and I watched the man to my left with interest as the minutes ticked by. One of the "inside men," a Sergeant with a walk-around bottle, tapped Eleven on the shoulder and asked him how many 4-cent stamps there were in a dozen. Eleven, full of confidence, scrawled the numeral 3 on his pad. "Last time I counted," said the Sergeant, "there were twelve stamps to the dozen." The remark was lost on Eleven, who was now quite hypoxic.

On the way back to sea level we stopped suddenly at 8,000 feet. Number Six, wide-eyed but calm, was holding one hand to the side of his face. Descent can play hell with sinuses, and Eight was in pain. The Sergeant was ready for this emergency and stepped past our boots to get to the student with a blocked maxillary. He tilted the man's head back and inserted the chrome nozzle of a spray gun into Eight's nostril, giving him a good spray of Neo-Synephrine. A few minutes later the mucous membranes contracted, allowing the trapped air inside the sinus cavity to escape, and Eight's face lighted up like those seen on television commercials.

The chamber was run back to earth and we unplugged from the consoles. But before we disconnected from the earphones there was one final reminder: "Have yourselves a good Valsalva before you go to sleep tonight." Some of the 100-percent oxygen we had been breathing for the past forty-five minutes would be absorbed by the tissues of the inner ear. Hours later, it would evolve from the tissues and build up pressure behind the eardrums. Give you a hell of an earache, if you didn't let it escape. Just pinch your nose and blow.

Students are given one other chamber flight toward the end of the program, when they are flying high in T-38s, and when this second ride is over, they are issued Form AF 1274, a red, wallet-sized card that is the admission ticket to flight above the three-mile limit in any airplane they can fly.

CHAPTER 6

THEY DON'T GO OVER
THE SIDE ANY MORE...

A few years ago, when the final kinks were being wrung out of the hot Century-series fighters, there was a saying among the fighter jocks that went, "There are two kinds of fighter pilots: those who have ejected, and those who will." Unfortunately, statistics seemed to bear this out. In 1959, 292 USAF aircrewmen ejected from their planes for one reason or another. In 1961, the total was 240; in 1962, 201. By 1964 the number of Air Force ejections around the world dropped to 93. Airplanes are becoming more reliable, and pilots are becoming more proficient, and had the U.S. remained in a state of relative peace, the number of ejections would have stabilized near the 100 mark. But with TAC fighter-bombers flying into radar-laid Russian flak batteries over Vietnam, the number of bail-outs has gone rocketing upwards. Until the war ends, and until airplanes become fail-proof, the possibility of having to make a sudden explosive egress from the cockpit is a specter riding every pilot's shoulder.

It can happen if the pilot can't get the gear down, or if there is a fire, or if the aircraft becomes uncontrollable, or if he runs out of fuel far from a prepared runway. And it can happen if the jet suffers a "double out," when both engines flame out and hydraulic boost to the control surfaces is lost. What was a swift metal arrow in flight, filled with thunder and fire, sensitive to every nuance of control input, becomes a thing of mush, mere tons of decelerating machinery with only marginal control. Such sick birds are not put down in the nearest pea patch, they are abandoned. The decision to eject must be reached within seconds.

One instructor warned, "If you are ever in a dead-stick

pattern in a Century-series fighter, your rate of descent will be anywhere from four to eight thousand feet per minute. This is in the neighborhood of 70 to 140 feet per second. If in this situation you waste five seconds trying for airstarts, you will lose upwards of 700 feet. Think about it."

It is during the height of such an emergency that a terrible conflict is set up within the pilot. He struggles between the desire to save the airplane by riding her down to a concrete runway and the urgent option of blasting clear. An airplane is something the pilot knows and loves. They are one, a man-machine team wedded to conquer time, distance, weather, and the enemy. The cockpit is home, the canopy a roof, the curved metal flanks his four walls of security. He is loath to desert this cocoon even though it is failing him badly.

During a series of low-level ejection tests conducted by the Research and Development Command, 200-lb. dummies were fired from heights ranging from 1000 feet down to runway level. The success rate was astonishing. Even the worst of the experimental systems enabled the dummies to ride to earth in a fully deployed chute from a firing level of only 100 feet. Dummies were separating from the seats in time—the equipment was working for *them*—but humans were still being killed and injured during emergency bailouts, and researchers wondered why. The answers were basic enough. During critical moments of stress pilots tensed like bowstrings, delaying positive action for fatal seconds, and some even rode their seats right into the ground, gloves tightly clenched to the armrests. A mechanical cure for the problem of seat retention was provided to *force* the pilot away from the

seat. Crossed straps running behind pilot and parachute
spring taut with a 125-lb. wallop that boots the pilot out
of the seat a split second after the gas-actuated lap belt
is automatically released. These man-seat separator straps,
known as "butt-snappers" to pilots, have saved many lives
over the years, but the psychological problem still remains.

This reluctance to abandon ship is evidenced in significant ways, even among green students. Instructors on
the ejection-seat training towers have remarked upon the
universal tendency for students to retain a tight grip on
the trigger handles even after the completion of the ejection cycle, i.e., at the simulated point when they would
be sprung clear by the separator straps. Pilots are re-
luctant to part with even the vestige of an airframe.

The "boom bucket," as the MH-15 ejection trainer is
called, stands just outside the door of the small building
housing Laughlin AFB's altitude chamber. Jutting twenty-
five feet into the air, the black tower dominates a yard
filled with the teaching equipment of survival. I thought of
guillotines and medieval torture devices and mangonels
when standing at the base of the tower, and I climbed
into the hot ejection seat with some apprehension. An
M-57 cartridge was placed in the trunnion block and the
firing head cocked. A red-streamered cotter safety pin was
slipped into the slide hole. The solenoid linkage was
attached, and while I tightened the shoulder harness, the
seat was slowly depressed on the rails hydraulically until
the seat was in full firing position.

I positioned my head against the back of the seat,
jammed my boots backward, and placed my elbows very
carefully inside the arm guards and located the dummy
controls inside the shadowed confines of the firing well.

"Pull safety pin!"

I reached down and withdrew the pin, placed it in the calf pocket of my flight suit, and zippered it closed. "Pin pulled," I shouted back.

"Throttle back!"

My left hand jerked back on the "throttle," a pale-green golf ball implanted on a shaft. "Throttle back."

"Activate bailout bottle!"

I jerked an imaginary green apple and screamed, "Octivate bailout battle!" This drew a guffaw from the watchers —and from me; nervousness in the face of a new experience is part of the game.

"Jettison canopy!"

Both hands reached for the seat handles, and I pulled hard. The arm guards came *kerchung!* up into place, and I was set for firing.

"Bailout!"

Any hesitation would mean hesitation forever. I grabbed the triggers and squeezed.

BLAM! The detonation of the shell crashed against my ears and my nostrils filled with cordite fumes. A mule-kick force walloped me smoothly up the rails and the seat braked to a stop five-tenths of a second later, fourteen feet up the rails. It was cranked down, and I got out without even a bruised coccyx.

Once students see how easy it is to get out of an airplane in trouble, they are shown how easy it is to get back to earth safely underneath the billowing canopies of their parachutes. Veteran instructors, most of them jump-rated, demonstrate parachute landing falls from a four-foot platform into a bed filled with gravel. Then the students line up and practice these PLFs again and again. Elbows together, fists covering their face, they leap from the platform and smack against the gravel with boots together and knees flexed. They land on the balls of their feet and immediately begin to roll right, left or backward, distributing the impact along calf, thigh, and buttock. The air is filled with thumps, bumps, and grunts for the better part of an hour before moving to the swing trainers where students practice manipulating the risers this way and that, practicing how to maneuver a parachute canopy away from power lines, trees, or buildings, and how to steer the canopy into the wind before landing, so as not to be dragged backwards along rocky terrain.

Then the action moves to a broad grassy field where six men, a couple of parachutes, and a half-ton pickup truck are waiting. This is the parasailing training ground, where students experience falling to earth from 500 feet under a parachute canopy that is opened before leaving the ground.

USAF has long realized that pilots look upon jumping out of airplanes as an unnatural act. The more hours a man spends in the cockpit, the stronger this feeling becomes. Yet there are times when it comes to either trusting your life to a parachute or sacrificing it in a futile attempt to stick with the bird. Parasailing was borrowed from the French, who developed it to train their own paratroopers in Morocco. It is USAF's answer to the uneasy questions students ask themselves, *Will the damn thing work? Is the landing hard?*

I watched nineteen consecutive parasailings in a six-knot wind, and more than half of the landings were made standing up. It looked like fun, and I had the chance to find out for myself one hot morning at Laughlin. I slipped on a helmet and standard parachute harness, and a

A parachute is sometimes a pilot's passport to survival. How to greet the earth is taught with bumps and groans.

Parasailing: taking the fear out of the unknown.

webbed tow yoke was snapped into the front risers. A
half-inch Dacron rope was secured to the yoke, a rope
that stretched 900 feet through the grass to the pickup
truck waiting down the field with engine idling. Behind
me, sergeants held on to the edges of the red-and-white
slotted canopy. I placed my boots apart and grabbed
the front risers with both gloved hands. "Remember,"
Captain Pendergras said, "start running when the truck
moves out. When you get airborne, hold your hands
behind your back. Keep your feet together. Don't look at
the ground. Keep your eyes on the horizon."

Pendergras stepped out of the way and picked up a bull-
horn. "Let 'er go!" he shouted. I was suddenly jerked
forward as the pickup began to accelerate into the wind.
I heard a pop as the chute deployed behind me, and I
started running. Three or four long strides and I was
airborne, still kicking my legs. The ground fell away and
I began to loft into the sky, feeling the great tension on
the risers. My body began to oscillate in swinging arcs
from side to side. I dropped my hands behind my back
and slid my boots together. There was only the whistling
of the wind in my ears and the flapping of the loose ma-
terial on the flight suit and those tiny figures falling farther
and farther away beneath my feet. The chute billows out
behind you and cannot be seen. There is the eerie sensation that you are being dragged skyward at the end of the
rope, without visible means of support.

The swaying motion stopped and I reached the top of
the parabola, 500 feet above the ground. I could see the
pickup truck, now no larger than a child's toy, bouncing
through the dry grass, leaving a trail of dust in its wake.
And I could see the tiny figures of men waiting to surround

me when I came back to earth. The truck slowed, and I began to descend. There were shouts from the ground, but all I could hear was the sighing of the wind. My boots were together, knees flexed. I grabbed the risers and kept my eyes on the horizon that suddenly began to rise. The truck and the running men grew lifesize again and my boots plumped against the ground. The rope was disconnected from the stanchion bolted to the bed of the pickup truck, freeing the rope. I hit the quick-releases on the harness, collapsing the chute. First reaction: let's do it again. This tow-up and tow-down is given students before they are hauled to altitude and cut loose from the rope to fall with the canopy directly overhead, as it would be during an emergency bailout. The canopy is 28 feet in diameter and made of a special non-porous nylon that slows the descent to 13 feet per second, offering ample time for the jumper to practice steering directly into the wind and to get the feel of damping oscillations by hauling on the proper risers.

To students who have parasailed, the prospect of an emergency bailout no longer holds unknown terrors. It is the unknown that nurtures fear, which in turn breeds fatal hesitation. Students learn that drifting slowly to earth under a canopy is an exhilarating experience, and when executed by the book is probably safer than crossing a busy street. They occasionally witness what happens when you forget everything you've been taught about canopy steering and the right way to do a PLF. An hour after my own ride, a student named Landon made every mistake in the book. He forgot to keep his boots together. He stared directly at the earth rushing up to meet him. Unnerved, oblivious to the shouts booming up at him from the men on the field who could see what was about to happen, he lifted one leg high—as though to postpone the inevitable—and absorbed the full impact with the other. The leg snapped above the boot top. Landon lost a class, but he will go on to parasail again, a wiser man.

Proof of the efficiency of the ejection-seat and parasail training was dramatically given during a routine T-37 acrobatic training flight in the summer of 1966. The student, Lieutenant Dick Price, and his instructor were aloft practicing spin recovery. The T-37 got itself into an inverted spiral, and despite the instructor's best efforts would not come out. Upside down, the cockpit occupants watched the earth swirl around faster and faster. Price heard through his earphones the command to bail out.

His hands flew. He jerked the green apple, disconnected from the primary oxygen supply, reconnected the zero lanyard, slammed his boots backward against the seat, shoved his helmet against the headrest and heaved on the armrests to raise the elbow guards. He positioned his elbows and heard the canopy pop loose and disappear. The instructor had already come off power, but Price was amazed at the force of the windblast that smashed against his visor. With the canopy gone, Price unhesitatingly grabbed the triggers and was shot out of the gyrating T-37 upside down, 12,500 feet over the spinning Texas countryside. His instructor punched out right afterwards.

One second after Price ejected, his seat belt automatically opened, and two-tenths of a second later the butt-snappers kicked him clear of the seat. The lanyard pulled the D-ring, and just 4.2 seconds after Price had squeezed the triggers, his chute cracked open and he was drifting down through the warm summer sky. Both

men landed unharmed and were back at Laughlin that afternoon being checked out by the flight surgeon.

"How was it, Price?"

Price grinned and replied. "No sweat. We are drilled hard on procedures; I knew what to do. Besides, I had great confidence in my equipment."

And that is precisely what this kind of training for emergencies is all about.

CHAPTER 7

THE 6,000-POUND
DOG WHISTLE

An alarm shatters the predawn stillness with the subtlety of an exploding hand grenade. Second Lieutenant Walter J. Brambille, twenty-three, reaches with a practiced hand and strangles the Westclox. Its radium-etched face glows sickly green with the time, 0430 hours. Small groans and full-blown yawns come from other beds in the bachelor officers' apartment. Jerry Crossen, a New Yorker, rolls out of the sack and while still not fully awake hefts barbells to add tone to an already impressive set of muscles. Arve Heggem, only nineteen and a NATO trainee from Norway, is first into the head to razor a teen-age beard. The shower is turned on full bore, beating a tattoo against the tin sheathing. The stereo is switched on and turned up; a crash of Tijuana Brass drowns out the thrumming of the air conditioner. From a test stand at the far end of the flight line a J-85 engine detonates into life, its anguished howl rolling like waves of thunder to beat against walls and windows, waking sleeping dogs and rushing birds into flight. Thus another training day begins while pinpoints of stars still gleam in a warm velvet sky.

Thirty minutes later the bachelor students are seated inside Laughlin's Officers' Club fiercely attacking rubbery fried eggs and burnt bacon twisted in agonized black shapes. The coffee, pilots swear, exceeds S.A.E. viscosity specs for hydraulic fluid.

Vast amounts of time and money have been spent to find ideal diets for pilots. Career fields have opened up for nutritionists in the Air Force. Pilots are provided the finest aircraft to use as tools of their trade. Yet, there never seems enough money to hire or train dedicated cooks to whip up palatable staples—and never mind gourmet dishes with the stamp of *cordon bleu*. Breakfast in the O

Club at Laughlin was something to be gotten over with quickly, like needed medicine. Students bitch less than older heads, probably because their minds are aswim with the nettlesome and exciting challenges of flying that crop up from minute to minute. Topic A in a gathering of student pilots is flying, not sex, and chow runs a poor third. Still, a really well-prepared breakfast has never been charged with handicapping a pilot whose day is filled with one long sweat of one kind or another. Curt LeMay knew this. The first task he set himself when he acquired SAC was to jack up the mess officer and the cooks of a strategic bombing wing whose performance was borderline.

Following the joust with breakfast, the student pilots deploy—Brambille to a briefing room near the flight line, Heggem to the Link Trainer building and Crossen to a class on the principles of flight, which he has been studying with the help of a 160-page programmed text. Programmed learning is used to teach every academic subject in the UPT curriculum. Most instructors and students swear by the method, an auto-instructional technique that has gained favor throughout a broad crosssection of the American educational system. Page 1 of the text explains just what programmed instruction is, and how a student can teach himself without leaping ahead to advanced knowledge. The page reads as shown on page 84.

Armed with a programmed text, the student can set his own pace of learning. His answer sheet is placed over the answer column on the right side of the page and he writes his answers there, checking responses as he goes. These programmed texts are used in and out of the classroom and are backed up by lectures, color sound films and slides. A few more samples from the text on principles of flight appear, starting with No. 16, on page 85.

1. This method of instruction will prob-   instruction
ably be new to you. It is called "pro-
grammed _____."

2. If your response to the above frame   answer, word
was "instruction," good for you. If you   or response
wrote anything else, draw a line   (any of the
through it, read the statement again   above are cor-
and write the correct response on your   rect)
answer sheet opposite the incorrect
_____ you marked out.

3. Always check the response you   a
wrote on your answer sheet to be sure
it checks with the correct answer that
appears.
    a. in the right column
    b. in the left column
    c. both
    d. neither

4. You have just answered another type   frame
of _____ which you will see
throughout this program.

5. The program will give you *cues* to   cue
help you respond to each frame cor-
rectly. A cue is something to "tip you
off" about the right answer. When a
word is underlined, it is a _____
to the right answer.

16. The rudder controls the aircraft about the *vertical axis*. This is called *yaw*. Yaw is movement about the:
    a. Longitudinal axis
    b. Vertical axis
    c. Lateral axis
    d. None of the above

vertical axis

17. The ailerons control movement about the longitudinal axis. This is called roll. Movement about the _____ axis is called roll and is controlled by the _____.

longitudinal
ailerons

Sometimes the information given is quite involved:

149. Using $F = Ma$, Newton's (a) _____ law, find the force required to accelerate an aircraft, with a mass of 200 slugs, 10 ft/sec².
    $F = (b)$

a. second

b. $F = 2000$ lbs

And—

150. Recalling that $M = \dfrac{W}{g}$, what acceleration would be achieved by applying a 4000 pound force to a 9600 pound aircraft?

$a = \dfrac{F}{M}$

$M = \dfrac{W}{g}$

$M = \dfrac{9600}{32} =$

    300 slugs

$a = \dfrac{4000}{300}$

$a = 13.3 \text{ ft/sec}^2$

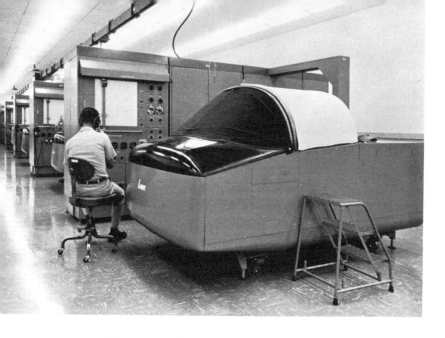

Mistakes made inside the Link are never costly.

However, neither of the above questions is as tough to answer as they may seem here, seen out of context. By the time the student works his way to 149 and 150, he will have learned the formulas and the definitions from preceding "frames" in the text. You cannot—unless you are already a graduate aeronautical engineer—skip ahead and still be able to stay with the game. You are forced to build your fund of knowledge one frame at a time.

While Crossen concentrates on filling in frames, Heggem has installed himself inside a large oblong box resting on an elevated platform, one of a series of such boxes aligned in a cab rank inside a huge air-conditioned building bristling with electronics. Heggem, dressed in boots, flight suit, and helmet, addresses a formidable array of instruments, dials, switches, circuit breakers, levers, buttons, and handles. He is face to face with the complicated consoles of a Cessna T-37B twin turbojet trainer aircraft. The Procedures Trainer, made by Link, can be flown to 35,000 feet without leaving the inside of the building. Every flight maneuver the T-37 is capable of executing in the air can be duplicated inside the close confines of the Link, and there is a realistic built-in feel to the flight controls. Heggem, like every other student, will spend 22½ hours inside the Procedures Trainer during the T-37 phase of his flight training. He will spend 3½ hours in the Link before coming to grips with the real airplane.

Seated to Heggem's right, in the instructor's seat, is an Airman 2/C, a hand-picked, highly trained specialist who will monitor Heggem's flight in the trainer. These enlisted specialists have developed a narrow skill that enables them to guide a student through certain phases of flight with as much proficiency as rated instructor-pilots. With IPs now at a premium, Airmen have had to take on increasing responsibilities in the Link, guiding students through parts of the training program usually restricted to IPs with hundreds of hours of jet time.

For an hour and fifteen minutes at a time students sit in the Link, learning where every last switch, control, and instrument is located. The goal is to reach automatically, without search, whatever switch or handle is needed to get the airplane off the ground, into the air, and back safely on the runway. The fat yellow checklist clipped to the left thigh pocket is the catechism of flight and is followed religiously, each item ticked off one by one. Skipping can lead to embarrassment. When "flying" the Link, I got in a hurry to reach 15,000 feet, rushing the procedures. Pitch attitude and indicated airspeed were correct, but the VVI (vertical velocity indicator) lagged far behind what was supposed to be an ideal rate of climb. I wondered why. The instructor jabbed his finger at an item on the checklist, one I had overlooked. "You've been climbing with 50-percent flaps since takeoff. You should've hauled them up when the IAS reached 110 knots. See? Item 3, page N-12."

Occasionally, green students have been known to rotate for a landing 3,000 feet beneath the surface of the earth, but it's better to do this in a Link than out of it, and mistakes made in the Link are usually mistakes remembered when aloft.

The progress of any Link flight can be monitored from outside the trainer as well as from within. The entire flight profile is traced with an ink stylus on a long strip of grid paper using a device mounted outside the cab. Thus an instructor can keep track of several students working their way through different assignments. He can observe, for instance, the telltale black line that reveals if a student has leveled off at 12,000 feet or has under-anticipated and come out forty or fifty feet high. There is no roar of engines, no turbulence or G forces to contend with, but a Link mission is remarkably realistic. Link time saves wear and tear on aircraft, saves money and—above all else— offers electronic life insurance. You can "crash" a Link and live to find out where you went wrong.

Down on the line, now washed by the warm rays of the rising sun, Walt Brambille and three others of Class 67-H are becoming acquainted with the airplane that will initiate them to the heady sensations of piloting small, twin-jet equipment. The left seat of this side-by-side trainer will be their home in the air for the next three months. They will learn to master the T-37 during daylight and at night, with an instructor and alone. With only thirty hours of light-plane time behind them, they are ushered into a trainer with performance characteristics equal to most first-line fighter planes of World War II.

The T-37 is fast, rugged, and forgiving. The broad metal wing can withstand a positive G load of 6.67, and the airframe can be pushed to Mach .7, or 382 knots, whichever comes first, before structural integrity is endangered. The engines are the small Continental J69-T-25 centrifugal-flow gas turbines developing 1,025 lbs. of thrust each. There are no afterburners. Three fuel tanks, one in each wing and one in the fuselage aft of the cockpit, hold 2,008 lbs. (309 gallons) of JP-4, affording the T-37 a cruising range of 650 miles. The wheel tread is a full fourteen feet, the belly rests low to the ground, the bulbous canopy

provides unexcelled vision over the short oval nose, and she touches down at a mild 85 knots; thus the airplane has been ideally designed for teaching students to land. The airplane shudders and shakes with St. Vitus's dance when approaching a stall, thus giving the pilot ample warning. The plane is beautifully acrobatic. The T-37 will spin like a dervish erect and inverted and recovers like any other airplane. Vertical (whip) stalls, snap rolls, and spins with excessive fuel tank imbalance are prohibited, and inverted flight for more than thirty seconds will flame out both engines; otherwise the airplane need never be treated with kid gloves. Fully fueled, a flight-ready T-37 grosses 6,575 lbs.

Although well-liked by pilots while in the air, the T-37 is an absolute torture machine while on the ground. One of the peculiarities of the J69 engine is the painful, ear-piercing shriek emitted by turbine blades whirling at a fantastic 21,730 rpm. The shrill intensity of this high-cycle scream will permanently damage unprotected eardrums, and pilots and ground crew are very careful about clapping plastic-and-foam "bunny ears" to their heads when approaching a T-37 that is winding up. From medium altitudes the T-37 sends back to earth a fluttery kind of whistle, and the airplane is often and affectionately called "Tweety Bird."

This oversize dog whistle rates high as a flying class-room, but is cursed with lack of creature comforts. The cabin is not pressurized; if you take her to 25,000 feet above sea level, then that is the altitude your bowels and sinuses must cope with. Earlier models were not blessed with air conditioning, and the AC units now installed are not as efficient as those on T-38s. It is not unusual to find midsummer runway temperatures of 95 or 100 degrees Fahrenheit in Texas. Strap on a heavy chute, encase your head in a plastic helmet, smooth your face inside an oxygen mask, truss yourself like a turkey inside the cockpit, lock tight the canopy—and you may as well be bound and gagged inside a reducing cabinet with heat lamps blazing full force. Sweat flows in torrents from every pore, sweeping past soaked eyebrows to sting the eyes. Sweat runs in channels on each side of the nose, dripping into the mask along with the usual drool.

You sit strapped inside the airplane, its metal skin too hot to touch, receiving the full treatment from an angry sun blasting through the transparent canopy. It is at such times, while cursing any delay in takeoff, that you wish the whole UPT operation could be transferred to northern Maine. For a few steaming minutes while still imbedded in the runway it is easy to develop a loathing for the Tweety Bird, but once away from the furnace, Earth, and climbing for altitude in cooler skies, you discover that you might very well take on the Tweet as a permanent mistress. She's responsive, obedient, and tolerant of small errors in handling.

Jet training gains momentum from the first day of instruction. By the end of the second week the student has logged six hours of dual. He has learned steep turns, precision turns, coordination exercises, slow flight, simulated traffic patterns and go-around at altitude, traffic pattern stalls, touch-and-go landings, full-stop landings and go-around from a low approach. The student and his instructor are assigned a work area all to themselves where the handling fundamentals can be practiced again and again until each nuance of movement of throttle and controls comes almost automatically. Throughout these flights, which last from sixty to eighty minutes, the instructor keeps up a running patter, taking the controls only to demonstrate or to show where a student has miscued.

While aloft, at briefings, at breakfast, lunch, and dinner, and at home in the evenings, emergency procedures are gone over and over again. What do I do if there is a sudden rise in the EGT temperature? If I see a fire warning light? If there is a sudden drop in oil pressure? If I lose hydraulic boost? If one or both engines flame out? If there is a compressor stall?

While at 17,000 feet one clear day over Laughlin, a student noticed the urgent red glare of the left engine fire warning light. The engine was shut down using the T-handle and by pulling back on the throttle. The light stayed on while descending through 7,000 feet, but there were no other indications of fire. A routine landing was made on one engine, and the T-37 was immediately towed to a maintenance hanger for a thorough checking. Investigation revealed the fire warning cables to be in good condition, but the overheat warning cable connectors were corroded, sending false information through the circuitry. The cables were replaced, the engine tested on the ground, and the T-37 was back in the air the next day.

Such routine, precautionary landings are made frequently. With four hundred sorties made every flying day at every UPT base, it is not surprising that somewhere, sometime, something will go wrong. What is surprising is that so few things do go wrong. A student may go through the entire training program, aging a year in the process, and never once experience equipment malfunction or face

The Tweet: introduction to the new and heady world of turbine flight.

any emergency. But he is drilled hard to react instantly if one does. Instructors are ready to show them how, despite the cost.

Early one morning in the fall of 1966, a T-37 climbed away from Reese AFB, near Lubbock, Texas. Two IPs were going up to visually check weather and flying conditions in the work areas to be used for the day's training. The jet climbed through 2,000 feet in calm air, and the IPs looked forward to an uneventful and pleasant thirty or forty minutes of flight in a sky just turning red with fire.

Suddenly the cockpit seemed to explode. A hurricane of wind roared through a large jagged hole torn in the right side of the windscreen. They had taken the full impact of a giant sandhill crane that had struck them head-on with a rate of closure of approximately 200 knots. The effect was no less lethal than a direct hit by flak. The IP sitting in the right seat was killed instantly. Blood, feathers, entrails, and excrement from the bird sprayed across what was left of the windscreen, across the top of the canopy, and throughout the cockpit. The pilot could have ejected, and nobody would have blamed him—except himself. He decided to bring his friend, the airplane, and himself home.

He automatically pulled off power to reduce airspeed to the minimum to keep flying, thus reducing the windblast that tore at his helmet and visor. He popped the speed brakes to hasten the rate of descent. Declaring an emergency, he turned back for the field and came straight in for a landing, past the rotating red beacons of the crash trucks, past the chunky little HH-43B helicopter waiting to take off in case of crash landing and subsequent fire. The T-37 was still topped off with fuel. The pilot, half-blinded, got gear and flaps down, speed brake up, and rotated for a good landing on the runway. This performance is testimony not only to one man's calmness, skill, and determination under duress, but also to a training system that builds reflexes which enable men to pull survival levers instead of pressing panic buttons.

Most students are ready for solo after fifteen hours of dual, and the lesson that precedes solo makes sure that the student is ready to take off and land the Government's three-ton airplane. This prep lesson is given usually on the twentieth flying day and is designed to build confidence in overcoming any number of sticky flying situations.

The airplane is lofted above 10,000 feet and brought straight and level. The instructor's voice crackling in your earphones tells you how to enter a full power stall. You clear the area, adjust the power setting to 90 percent and smoothly haul back on the stick, watching the attitude indicator and working with the rudder to prevent yaw. When the attitude indicator tells you that the T-37 is pitched up at 40 degrees, you hold her there, feeling the controls go slack as the stall approaches. You work harder now with rudder and ailerons to keep mushing straight ahead. Now the airframe begins to buffet as the wings are robbed of lift. You release back pressure and smoothly advance the throttles to 100 percent, still stabbing left-and-right at the rudder pedals. The nose comes down, and you feel the controls tighten as airspeed begins to build. Now you coordinate stick and throttle to bring the plane back straight and level at 90-percent power. Now you go through precisely the same motions, except this time you deliberately louse up the recovery in order to put the Tweet into a secondary stall. You haul back too soon and too quickly on the stick, and you let the throttles stay put at 100 percent. In rushing the recovery from the original stall you succeed in re-stalling. This teaches you that haste makes waste—and one thing you cannot afford to waste is altitude.

You put the T-37 into stalls in a no-flap configuration, with the nose low on a simulated final turn, at 200 knots with power cut back and with the airplane in a steep bank and in a slow-speed, nose-high attitude—all of which will teach you how to recover if you hit a stall while in any portion of the traffic pattern.

Probably no maneuver causes as much acute queasiness as the spin. And it's not so much the actual spin itself, but the thought of getting into one that accounts for a certain apprehension. The first one is the worst.

You fly to 18,000 feet and begin tidying up the cockpit. You stow any loose gear, tighten belt and shoulder harness to the limit, and check instruments to make sure the total fuel load is not above 1000 lbs. and that fuel imbalance is not more than 70 lbs. You trim out the airplane, clear the area, then begin the wild ride by violating the laws of stable flight. The nose is honked up to forty or fifty degrees of pitch and the stick moved hard to the left (if you are going to spin left). The wings clutch for lift, which is rapidly disappearing, and at the first sign of buffeting you vigorously punch down on left rudder while insulting the airplane with a steady back pressure on the stick. The plane gives up. It stops flying, and the nose falls back to vertical, rises again, then flops down through the horizon and the airplane begins its dervish rotation.

The world seems to go mad with spinning, and you feel that you are going to be shoved through the canopy. If it is the instructor who has put the airplane into the spin, you have a difficult time in telling whether the spin is to the right or to the left. With the rudder and stick held firmly to the limits of travel you will be in a stabilized spin losing 500 feet per turn, each turn lasting three seconds, with the nose pitched down 30 degrees. Four turns will make a visual stew out of earth, sky, and clouds and make you long for a return to a normal world. Getting out of a spin does not call for finesse. You stomp at the opposite rudder as though trying to clobber a rattlesnake. After one accelerated turn you shove the stick full forward and keep it there until the nose pitches down. When it does, ease off pressure on the stick, but keep your boot planted on right rudder until the world—or so it seems—stops gyrating. Then you neutralize the rudder and resume back pressure on the stick to bring the airplane out of the dive. The first spin experience is a nasty sensation, but after two or three times on the vertical merry-go-round you lose the initial sense of disorientation. What the student must always bear in mind is the fact that any aircraft can be stalled at any speed, depending upon its attitude, and that a combination of a stall and yaw will result in unintentional spinning of many, but not all, airplanes. Getting into a spin near the ground leaves the pilot no option except instant pulling of the "next-of-kin triggers."

There are times when even the best flight planning will result in coming home with minimum fuel on board. Under such conditions a missed approach or being told to go around by mobile control is potentially embarrassing.

To fly a normal 360-degree traffic pattern just might see you on the downwind leg with suddenly silent engines. A short, quick way down is provided by flying a closed traffic pattern. Gear and flaps are brought up, the nose is kept down, building up airspeed. The throttles are advanced to MIL and the pilot reefs the airplane around in a tight 45 to 60 degree bank, rolling level after 180 degrees of turn, headed on the downwind leg. Then the landing proceeds normally.

When these procedures (simulated forced landings have recently been dropped) have been mastered to the hard-eyed instructor's satisfaction, the student is told he is going solo the very next day. It might be in the morning, at noon, or in the afternoon; whatever the time, first jet solo is a shining milestone, a sharp wedge driven between any student pilot's past and his future.

This heady half-hour alone at the controls may consist of no more than three traffic patterns and landings, all eyeballed and binoculared by the IP from the little air-conditioned steel-and-glass RSU (runway supervisory unit) at the edge of the runway, but when the sweating student shuts down his engines and climbs from the vacant cockpit he feels twelve feet tall. It is a momentous event, and should be lustily celebrated. In the old days, soloists were flung kicking into the nearest—and preferably dirtiest —puddle of water available. The New Tigers are denied this privilege.

Lieutenant Burdin, explaining, allowed a note of nostalgia to creep into his voice when he recalled that Laughlin once was famous for "the muddiest, nastiest, gooiest, slimiest pool of mud in the state of Texas. That was our solo pool. Throw a student in there, suit, boots, and all, and it was something he remembered. Then some-body got the idea it wasn't dignified. It might have been all right for cadets, but not for commissioned officers. We filled in the mud. We started using the officers' swimming pool, but somebody else said we couldn't use *that* until a test was run by the lab people to make sure the chlorine content was high enough ... or maybe the guy had athlete's foot and we had to check *that* out. From solo to splash has to be a spontaneous thing. Who has time to ask for a mobile sanitation unit to come around with test tubes and a microscope on the greatest day in a student's life? We stopped using the pool."

"What happens now? Pour water on them out of a glass?"

"No. Come on, I'll show you."

We walked around to the rear of a wooden building near the flight line. Burdin pointed toward a collapsed yellow plastic bag sagging against the grass. Looking closer, I made out one of those kiddie waders you blow up and fill with water so two-year-olds can splash around without danger of drowning. Around the sides were sten-cilled in color various characters from the literary world of children. Captain Kangaroo for future death-dealing fighter pilots?

"Ah," Burdin said, "what are we trying to make here? Pussycats or tigers?"

Although the days when cadets double-timed from barracks to chow, from chow to flight line, from flight line to classroom are gone, the current breed of student is kept on the run nevertheless. From sunrise to sunset, and often beyond, meticulously worked out time schedules fill every working day. If a takeoff time is posted for 0716 hours, it does not mean 0718 hours. A class in aerodynamic engineering scheduled to begin at 0900 begins at 0900. A student who arrives at 0910 may discover that he has missed a lesson review and a three-minute pop quiz. Pressure is constant, relieved only by weekends, and those are broken by scattered hours spent hunched over programmed texts and flight manuals. There are no upperclassmen playing a noncom role, lashing students on with caustic tongues. Keeping up with the program requires self-initiated drive, and self-discipline is far more cruel than discipline poured down from above; it is a knot of anxiety and determination that gives a man no real peace.

Flight commanders and IPs realize that stress can cause a student to magnify a simple goof into a hideous error rising up to blot out his flying career. With so much at stake, anthills have a way of becoming Everests. However, the UPT program makes a sharp distinction between a lackadaisical attitude and occasional gaffes.

I watched how this distinction was made very early one morning following a weather briefing for the T-37 sorties that were laid on for the day. The flight commander laid his pointer down on a desk and called one student to attention. Then he summoned another flight-suited, burr-headed lieutenant forward. He carried a green brick in his hand. There was a formal little ceremony in which the brick changed hands, salutes were given, and the whole performance was greeted with whistles, catcalls, and a scattering of applause. The "Zunk Award" had been presented to a man whose goof that week was greater than the one committed by the previous honoree. The new Oscar winner found himself strapped in the left seat of a T-37, ready for taxi and takeoff. He suddenly realized he was not receiving radio transmissions from the IP, who had a

Pilots—and their IPs—are only human. Weekly Zunk Award is presented to T-37 students who have sinned but lightly.

strange look on his face. No wonder: the student still had his ear defenders clamped to his head; his helmet and oxygen mask were hanging on a peg back in the ready room.

Then there was Jennings, who completed a dual mission in a Tweet, shut down the airplane, unstrapped, and walked halfway back to the debriefing shack before he realized he had left his parachute in the airplane. When he went back and reached in to retrieve this important item of flight equipment, he failed to observe that the D-ring was fouled; so when he hefted the heavy bag upward, there was a spectacular cockpit deployment of seven hundred square feet of white nylon.

Those who truly love the sky are goners to passion two weeks after solo. Beginning with Contact Lesson Sixteen, one is allowed into the soaring, horizon-twisting, eyeball-oscillating, utterly exhilarating G-world of full aerobatics. Straight and level flight at altitude in calm air provides about the same physical sensations as cruising down a broad deserted Arizona highway in a Lincoln Continental; comfortable and relaxing, but not very exciting. It is when—as USAF puts it—you "exploit the entire perform-ance envelope of the aircraft" that you feel as though you were coming into your own as a pilot, that the airplane is doing what it was meant to do.

There are several reasons why, in an era of radar vector-ing to targets where precise, straight-on gunnery patterns are flown, aerobatics are still stressed. These reasons are spelled plainly for every student:

"The purpose of teaching you aerobatic maneuvers is to help you develop a more sensitive feel in handling the aircraft and to improve your ability both to coordinate the flight controls and to maintain full awareness of your orientation, regardless of attitude, and put the aircraft where you want it. Aerobatics will teach you to feel at ease when your body is oriented at any angle—and that you can think, plan, observe and perform as easily while inverted as while upright. Though having the ability to perform aerobatics is important within itself, the confidence you gain from performing these maneuvers is equally important."

Or, as put by a student: "Acro is fun, and I feel like I can fly that mother out of any attitude at any speed over any given point and come out on top every time." Confidence . . . that's what the manual says.

Doing acro with precision is an art that is developed from painstaking attention to craftsmanship over a very long period of intensive practice. The pilots of the Thunderbirds and the Blue Angels are the highest practitioners of the art. But to perform acrobatics *fairly* well requires only close attention to the IP's instructions, a basic sense of timing, and a supreme disregard of the fact that you are enclosed inside a winged capsule whipping through the sky twice as fast as a Le Mans Ferrari and moving in three directional axes—sometimes canted, sometimes inverted, sometimes pointed straight down, sometimes straight up, and almost always pulling G.

One of the famous combat maneuvers of World War I and World War II was the split S, sometimes spelled "split ess" and known to RAF pilots as "split arse." It was sometimes used to shake an enemy off your tail, but it eats up a lot of sky and is taught USAF student pilots early in the game so they will know how *not* to recover

from inverted flight. You begin by trimming up the air-craft, using the little black plastic button on top of the stick. If, after the climbout past 5,000 feet, you find steady back pressure needed to keep the nose level, you nudge the trim button backward once or twice. Elevator trim tabs, electrically activated, obediently drop downward. Dynamic pressure of airflow against the tabs deflects the entire elevator surface upwards and can be held in the slipstream without force. With power set at 90 percent, and with a careful search of the sky to make sure you are clear, you are ready to split-ess.

The stick is eased back until the nose reaches a 30-degree pitch attitude. Quick, now, take your eyes off the attitude indicator and flick your eyes left and right to make sure the wings are level; a low wing, high pitch attitude, and bleeding off of airspeed combine to set up conditions for a stall and unintentional spinning. Back on the airspeed indicator, and when she drops to 120 KIAS, trip the little switch on the right throttle that retracts the speed brake, while pushing the stick over to get the Tweet inverted with wings level. Now begin back pressure on the stick that drops the nose and sees the horizon plummet upward and disappear. Max pressure is held until the horizon comes up again, then is eased in time to come straight and level on a reciprocal heading.

The first few times, it doesn't always come out that way. While in a rolling climb it is easy to become disoriented at the point of anticipating opposite aileron to come level; too much and you slide off to the right, too little and you slither down to the left. You get angry with yourself for lousing it up, and wish you could get out of the airplane and observe from a distance what, exactly, you are trying to make the airplane do. You keep at it until the initial

Night finds Brambille and Heggem hangar flying, seeking dates and, above all, studying long hours.

disorientation disappears and until you have a clear idea of the track the airplane describes in the sky.

And so it goes through high-speed dive recovery, loops, barrel rolls, aileron rolls, Immelmanns at 270 knots with 3G seat pressure, the dizzy cloverleaf and Cuban 8s, which is a modified combination of a loop and an Immelmann. Acro is the most sensational part of flying, especially in jets, which respond to the pilot's every control option with a smoothness found in no other type of aircraft. Acro, besides teaching pilots how to put an airplane where they want it, and when, is USAF's most potent antidote for brains cobwebbed with the academic load.

The contact (VFR) phase of T-37 instruction is divided into twenty-nine dual and thirteen solo sorties for a total of 55:40 hours. Then follow seventeen dual instrument missions totaling 22:40 hours, five dual sorties to provide 7:40 hours of basic navigation procedures, and four formation flights of an hour each. There is some quarrel with the IPs about this, who believe four hours of formation work is simply not enough. Formation work is, and has always been, tricky and demands the utmost of coordination and anticipatory reflexes. Tight formation flying by students is potentially hazardous, but *not* flying tight formation in a tactical combat situation is more dangerous still.

It was getting along toward eight o'clock in the evening, and we were sprawled in various attitudes among the overstuffed couches and chairs in the bachelor apartment shared by Brambille, Crossen, and Heggem. The students had enjoyed a long, hard day of flying—in the air and inside the Link—classroom work, and laps around a quarter-mile track to comply with the 5BX Plan for Physi-

cal Fitness. They were, in fact, fairly pooped. The sugges-
tion that we dine at the O Club was vetoed; instead we
piled into a faded two-tone '59 Chevy and drove to a
roadside pizza stand between Laughlin and Del Rio and
came back to the barracks loaded with pizzas.

While we licked gooey mozzarella from our fingers,
words spilled out describing attitudes, reactions, and
motivations. Yes, there was no doubt that the Air Force
provided the finest instructors and the best airplanes—but
the Navy flight suits, gloves, and helmets were better. No,
the USAF survival knife with its orange handle and
hooked blade to make the four-line cut on chute risers
was certainly not an example of Old World craftsmanship;
the steel of the blades was definitely not from Solingen.
Yes, the curriculum of the entire program was refined to
its probable limit; the dovetailing of academics, Link, and
actual air work could hardly be better from a learning
standpoint. True, the AC on the Tweet could stand a hell
of a lot of improvement . . . but wasn't it great to fly? No,
you would not find better guys anywhere than in the UPT
program.

Crossen, whose father drove hot, skittish Martin B-26s
against the Japanese during World War II, inherited all
the motivation needed to survive current USAF pilot
training. Brambille, a chemistry major from the College of
St. Thomas in his native Minnesota, knew what he wanted
from the first day of training: "To fly the hottest thing
they've got."

As to the deeper reason why each of these men had
chosen a career as a military pilot was probably nutshelled
by Heggem with an unabashedness typical of Norwegians.
He said, "Why, man, it's my whole life!"

CHAPTER 8

NO MEDALS, NO GLORY

The hardest-working—yet most unsung—man in the entire pilot training program is the instructor. To the student, no one besides himself is as important as the taskmaster who sits at his right in a T-37, and a few feet behind him in a T-38. A dedicated IP can extract the full potential from a brilliant learner and can elevate a timid "fair" to a confident "good." On the other hand, a bored IP can tarnish gold, and his borderline cases are doomed to a series of check rides that usually lead to elimination. The first time a student straps himself in the cockpit he is filled with three parts anticipation and one part apprehension that he struggles to control. His unspoken questions, logically inspired, seldom vary: *Is this IP with his hundreds or thousands of hours really interested in teaching me to fly, or could he care less that I might wind up among the twenty percent programmed for elimination?* When the first sortie is over and the plane shut down, the student will have his answer. It may take years, but eventually the truth dawns: the student–IP relationship, which lasts for 186 days in basic and advanced, will affect the new pilot's attitude toward the cockpit and USAF as a whole for the length of his military career.

To appreciate fully the rigid procedures under which instruction is given today it is necessary to glance backward briefly to another era. During World War II, pilot production reached its peak in December 1943, when 74,000 cadets were undergoing various phases of flight instruction.* The wash-out rate was seldom less than

* On September 3, 1939, when the world was once again plunged into global war, there were only 2007 rated pilots in the entire regular Army Air Corps. Pilot production to that time averaged less than 200 per year.

forty percent, and fatalities were common. Instructors, then as now, were pulled into Training Command after completion of a tour of combat, and they came directly from pilot training centers after receiving their wings and commissions. That most of the men chosen as instructors were good pilots there is little argument. But a good pilot is not necessarily a good instructor; possessing knowledge and technique, and being able to transmit them to others, are two separate qualities. During the war, and for a long time afterwards, there were no set procedures for instruction; the book on how to be a successful IP had yet to be written. One instructor had one method of trying to make a military aviator out of a green cadet; another IP had his own techniques. No two approaches were ever the same. Some IPs had reputations as holy terrors; their mission in life (or so it seemed to students) was to lean so hard on students that they were popped out of the program from sheer pressure.

Lieutenant Colonel Frank Hammock, Command Briefer for ATC, recalls one instructor the students knew as "Old Iron Butt." Hammock, a cadet in 1943, was having difficulties in holding straight and level during the contact phase of basic. Up front in a low-wing BT-13, Hammock inched stick and rudder this way and that, not quite getting it. Iron Butt spoke through the gosport tube in surprisingly gentle tones. "Hammock, give me the controls. I think you're missing it because you have no clear understanding of the mechanical linkages involved. Lower your head and look closely at the cables underneath your feet. Watch as I move the controls, now." Hammock innocently lowered his head, covered only by the thin leather helmet, and peered closely at the cables and linkages, which were exposed to view. Suddenly the stick beat a vicious tattoo of blows against the top of his head. *Wham! Bam! Bam!*

"There, you stupid sonofabitch!" the instructor roared. "Maybe that'll teach you to pay attention." Hammock's headache lasted the rest of the day as a reminder, but the incident served more to heighten his anger at the IP than it did to teach him the fine points of flight.

During and after the Korean War—which the Government still refers to as "conflict," an empty name to cover the deeds of nearly 40,000 American dead—the operating word in USAF was "Tiger." The spirit of competitive aggressiveness permeated the total structure of the Air Force, beginning with a man's first day in the cadet program and continuing through combat in the skies south of the Yalu. The motto, *Every Man a Tiger,* was shouted lustily by cadets double-timing to the flight line and was seen printed on signs stuck over washbasin mirrors, in briefing huts, and in academic classrooms. Determined F-86 pilots of one squadron loved to get the drop on other F-86 or F-84 pilots, bouncing them from out of the sun at 30,000 feet or screaming across their airfields in a subsonic dash a hundred feet off the deck. This aggressiveness, coupled with superior flight training, paid off; the kill ratio of Sabres over MIG-15s was fourteen to one. USAF's accident rate was also high: you can't put claws on a tiger without shedding blood.

The tiger motto slowly faded away. The operating word today is "professionalism," and the entire philosophy of ATC instruction is based on making every pilot a real pro. He is taught to fly by the book, a comprehensive set of procedures painstakingly worked out through the years designed to cover every conceivable flight situation. Scott

Crossfield, one of the world's great rocket test pilots, once said that he has never been frightened in the air during any emergency "because I have never run out of things to do," which is justification enough for flying by a book that always gives pilots something to do when things start coming unglued.

The dangers inherent in Prussianizing flight instruction are recognized. Teaching students to fly by manuals, graphs, charts, and rigid procedures without turning them into robots who fly mechanically requires crossing very fine lines on the part of IPs. To turn out a pilot with instincts as well as cold procedural knowledge demands that the IP become what is termed "a manager of human resources." That is, the instructor must accurately gauge his student and know how to extract his full capabilities. Psychology is every bit as important a tool to the IP as anything in the ATC inventory.

Phrases such as "escape mechanism," "projection," "error of central tendency," and "the developmental approach" would have been about as familiar to the average World War II instructor as incantations from an Urdu fertility rite. Yet these are everyday working phrases in the IP's lexicon of today; he has come to grips with the *Gestalt* of the student flier. IPs are schooled in the technique of positive and negative motivation to extract maximum performance from every student. The manual states that positive motivation is always preferred, but sarcasm can "sometimes" be used if the IP is certain that the student knows he is being "kidded for his own good." Ridicule is prohibited, but mild fear can occasionally be employed to drive home a point if that point has to do with a threat to life or matériel.

Captain Gaillard Peck, Jr., was debriefing a student of

IPs have every modern, expensive aid to help drive home knowledge, but man-to-man critiques provide ultimate answers to classroom and cockpit problems.

the Pilot Instructors' School, where USAF teaches combat veterans and recent UPT graduates everything that is known about becoming an IP. "Okay," Peck said, "you held formation pretty good in there, and your re-joins after element separation were smartly executed. But look here." Stabbing a pencil point against a chart, Peck showed where the student—acting as element leader—had mistimed his turn over a road. "You took us ten degrees off on that turn . . . we just got our butt shot down by the enemy." The thought that lack of aggressiveness with aileron might one day cost him his life had not occurred to the "stud," who nodded and filed away the comment for future reference.

"Suppose," Peck continued, "we took a bird strike while in the pattern. The canopy's cracked and there's blood and crap all over the place. What would you do?"

"Stick my head out of the hole in the canopy and go ahead and turn on final?" the student suggested hopefully.

"At 175 knots?"

"Yeah, I guess you're right. Wouldn't work."

"How about calling for a GCA? Or if you can see out either side, landing with your wingman?"

"Sure, that's right. I could do that."

"Don't sweat it," Peck said. "That's what you're here for, to learn."

USAF's 3510th Flying Training Group runs a special school for future IPs at Randolph AFB. Pilots who have never served as instructors spend ten weeks in the cockpit and in academics, and former IPs are upgraded in six. Long-course students graduate after sixty hours of flying time and sixty-four hours of classroom work. Student input is derived from pilots who have transferred from other commands, from men fresh out of pilot training themselves, and from pilots only weeks out of the combat zone in Southeast Asia. Thus, Peck may carry as students a thirty-two-year-old captain who has flown 2000 hours in transports, a twenty-four-year-old second lieutenant recently graduated from Laughlin with 240 hours total, and a thirty-year-old captain who has spent years as a fighter pilot and who is a hundred-mission man over North Vietnam flying F-100s. Each of these types faces a different set of problems in learning to become an IP.

For the old head whose experience has been limited to many-engined airplanes, the T-38 is a whole new flight experience; it has been years since he graduated from single-engined jet T-33s. Not only must be become completely proficient in the airplane, he must leave behind him years of experience that do not conform to the rigid Air Training Command procedures. One such captain remarked: "I have learned a whole lot of the tricks of the trade since I've been flying during the past ten years. Some short cuts for this and that, techniques for recovering from situations in flight, little ways of doing things that save time or effort. Well, almost all of this has to be forgotten by me in order to conform to the way things are done in ATC. I can see the benefits of standardization —there's no question about that—but it's hard to shear off all these rough edges of experience. It's like starting off all over again."

The process of conforming is easiest for the new UPT graduate, who has just spent fifty-three weeks obeying rules. But his problem is adapting to a complete reversal of roles in only ten weeks. For more than a year he has

IPs are made, not born. For each hour aloft many more are spent planning the day's missions.

been in a student frame of mind; IPs were minor gods who led the way, who could be depended upon to salvage a flight that he, the student, may have allowed to deteriorate to the point of fiasco. Now, with hardly a pause for transition, yesterday's student is today's IP with heavy responsibility.

Sixty hours of flying per week is a lot, and all of it is spent by student IPs riding the back seat of the T-38. Up front is another IP, alert to every lapse in procedure during the flight. The student IP plans the mission, conducts the briefing, leads the whole show. Afterwards his performance is dissected to lay bare every fault.

Up until the winter of 1966, almost all the instructors at the PIT school at Randolph were UPT graduates who had gone through the school themselves, then had gone off to one of the ATC bases to instruct, then were sent back to teach others to instruct. First Lieutenant Al Taylor, of the 3514th PIT Squadron is one example. Taylor graduated from the University of Omaha with an ROTC commission, then got his wings at Williams AFB in Arizona in December 1963. He learned to instruct, then spent time at Laredo AFB on T-37s. Now he's back at Randolph, teaching others to become IPs. Taylor sits in the right side of a Tweet, passing along the benefit of his 1300 hours in the air to others, and he finds it a constant challenge. Gail Peck agrees. Peck, an Air Force Academy graduate, grew up in the Air Force: his father once commanded the Pilot Training Wing at Laredo AFB. After an exhilarating flight in a T-38—Peck was helping get a lieutenant colonel IP qualified—we came down and feasted on typical pilot fare, coffee and cheeseburgers.

U.S. AIR FORCE T-38A NO.3
A.F. SERIAL NO.60-565

SUITABLE FOR USE OF AROMATIC FUEL
SERVICE THIS AIRCRAFT WITH GRADE
JP-4 FUEL IF NOT AVAILABLE T.O. NO.
1T-38-1-1A WILL BE CONSULTED FOR
EMERGENCY ACTION

STATIC PORT

Formation work: follow the leader at 500 knots.

"The thing is," Peck said, "is to be able to keep your perspective when guys keep screwing up in the air. I don't get many who really make gross errors, but it's all the small things—things I suppose I take for granted after years as an IP. I have to keep reminding myself that the guy sitting there behind me is probably trying his damnedest to hack it, that he's got his mind on trying to fly the airplane, on procedures, and on trying to please me so we'll have a good debrief. He is trying to develop his own patter so that it comes out automatically, leaving his attention free to monitor. Unconscious, really, of what he is saying. It takes a lot of concentration to learn to divide your mind that way."

As the war goes on, pilots like Peck and Taylor will be moved out to transition into combat. The combat men they have trained will eventually find their way back to the PIT school, and they, in turn, will be teaching other combat men to become IPs. Within a year or two, new student pilots at ATC bases will be gaining the direct benefit of IPs who have already "met the elephant" and have lived to pass on their experience in hot air warfare.

IPs work hard. Although students at ATC bases can occasionally lounge around in the sack until 0530, IPs more often than not are already down at the line by that time going over the day's schedule and reviewing the different lessons each of their students must go through that day. Scheduling is a complicated procedure involving such factors as availability of aircraft (itself a maintenance factor), student requirements, weather, and air space—always at a premium. All takeoffs from any UPT base are given numbers and times. At Laughlin, for example, the "Roy Bean" schedule lists the first takeoff at

0600, the second at 0604, the third at 0607, and continues throughout the day until takeoff number 275 at 2159 hours. The IP must fit in his students' day somewhere within that time block, making sure the mission, contact or instrument, does not interfere with any other of the gaggle of T-37s and T-38s constantly taking off, climbing out, doing acro in designated areas, in the traffic patterns or on final.

Of course, the IP has help. With the aid of an IBM 1401 computer and a stack of cards, one for each student pilot, flight scheduling has never been done faster. Under the old manual system, more than 1800 separate factors had to be considered and assimilated to determine each day's succeeding operation. IPs and scheduling officers spent more time—a lot of it inefficiently—in this burdensome and irksome paper work than they did in the cockpit or in briefing. The computer system, known in USAF as the Automated Student Management System, has stored all prerequisite and special instructions associated with each lesson in the syllabus. This data is applied to each student in turn by the computer, which determines a valid list of flying options which each student is eligible to receive. A by-product of the ASMS is that the computer provides a permanent data bank that can be used for statistical analysis whenever needed to measure any student's progress, or to check overall program effectiveness. On one card, then, the IP has the following information instantly available: what lesson his students can be opted for that day, the student's flying time, and on which lessons the student has received a Fair or an Unsatisfactory grade.

At Laughlin, as at most of the other UPT bases, IPs carry as many as four students each—which is two more than the absolute ideal. IPs rack up a lot of cockpit time, but very little pilot time: the student does 90 percent of the stick-and-throttle work. The IP is a teacher, not an executor, and as a teacher he bears the responsibility for grading his students on every phase of piloting, and these grades have a lasting influence on the student's career. The IP must avoid the lure of marking everything *Good* or *Satisfactory* where performance is concerned; it may be difficult to justify an *Excellent,* and it requires a thick skin to check off *Unable* against the record of a man who works hard, who wants to be a military pilot more than anything else. The IP has to guard against "Error of Halo": marking a student high because they are from the same town, attended the same university, or share the same tastes. He has to watch for a tendency to match the worst of his students against the best, i.e., use his own four students as a narrow-range gauge instead of grading each man against the standards of the whole UPT program. An IP, then, should combine the qualities of an under-standing, kindly uncle in order to draw the student out— then be able to grade a performance with cold, emotionless detachment. It is never easy.

Occasionally, the IP faces checks on his own perform-ance from detached-looking pilots from the Standards Evaluation Board. These Stan Eval people, all experienced airmen, climb inside the airplane with the IPs and request that a training mission be flown—and woe to the IP who uses some of his own peculiar techniques in lieu of those found in the manuals, or short-cuts a checklist in order to get wheels up at the appointed time. Stan Eval is there to make sure the training program is run strictly according to the book; they are watchdogs of procedure.

Being an IP requires patience, an understanding of human nature, an eye for painstaking detail, and physical stamina. They go to work before dawn, fly two or three sorties a day, and must go through four and six briefings and post-flight critiques and attend to hours of paper work. They go home after dark, too pooped to care about much more than a hot shower, chow, and the blessed luxury of doing absolutely nothing. It is a life of coping with routine mixed with no small amount of frustration. There are no special decorations for IPs, the make-or-break pilots of the whole training program, but there is the reward of seeing a promising student fulfill your every expectation, of being able to resurrect a stud teetering on the abyss of failure and watching him graduate, after all.

Captain Samuel E. Armistad, of Ramer, Alabama, put his finger directly on the matter of IP satisfaction. Armistad has flown more than 1500 hours in F-100s, including a combat tour in Vietnam with the 531st Tactical Fighter Squadron. Armistad left TAC to become an IP, a job he volunteered for. "I look at it this way," he said. "My job is important to the Air Force, to the country, and especially to all those younger guys I'm training to become pilots. And every time I send a man solo, I feel that a little bit of me is up there with him. And wherever he flies in the years to come, I'm still there as a silent co-pilot, ready to get him home safely if he gets into an emergency situation. It's a good feeling, believe me."

CHAPTER 9

THE WHITE ROCKET

I n March 1961, USAF accepted delivery of the first production T-38 to roll off the Northrop assembly line in Southern California. This clean, arrogant machine rested lightly on three tiny wheels pressing against the concrete apron at Randolph AFB, then a UPT base. The considerable crowd that gathered around the angular, tense-looking Talon, as the factory had named it, were all professional blue-suits. Among them was Colonel Charles E. Yeager, who had dazzled the world earlier by flying the all-rocket Bell X-1 to the unprecedented speed of Mach 1.4. The plane Yeager now looked at was no research tool to be entrusted to visionary test pilots; it was a supersonic trainer—the world's first—designed to be flown by kids. And it was only one-twentieth of a Mach number slower than the X-1.

The T-38 was, and is, unique in that it was a product of a team effort shared by a civilian contractor and a special task force of hand-picked Air Force officers, most of them pilots with a wide range of aerodynamic and engineering backgrounds. The T-38 would be designed from scratch to replace the venerable Lockheed T-33, the subsonic single-engine jet that Korean War fighter pilots had used as a basic trainer. Students graduating out of the T-Bird into cockpits of heavy supersonic tactical combat aircraft were taking too long to adjust to the new environment. There was a long time-lag before pilots became fully proficient at the controls of Century-series fighters, time that could have been more profitably utilized in learning weapon system delivery techniques. The T-38 was conceived in order to cut pilot combat readiness time by providing them with an airplane with most of the characteristics of first-line aircraft, but with as few of their vices as possible. The USAF T-38 Project Team already knew, in outline, what the new trainer's specs must include: supersonic capability, two engines, high sink rate, high rate of climb, and high-altitude true airspeed navigation. These were basic; further refinements were compiled after exhaustive studies of ATC maintenance and operational and flight safety reports. Among them:

1. Improved audio and visual landing-gear warning system.

2. Logical placement of instruments and radios on the instrument panel to prevent spatial disorientation.

3. Staggered location of flight-control quick disconnects making it impossible to cross-connect cables that would inadvertently reverse action of flight controls.

4. Varying sizes of hydraulic disconnect fittings to obviate dangerous cross-connections.

5. Either engine made capable of supplying hydraulic power for aircraft flight-control operation, i.e., if one engine flames out, the other provides a backup system of power boost.

6. Controls designed to enable aircraft to be flown and landed safely while using only one aileron.

7. Installation of selective-position speed brakes on underside of fuselage to permit unusually rapid descent from altitude and to reduce airspeed to within safe margins.

8. Cockpit controls placement-designed so no controls are located aft of pilot's elbow.

9. Improved visibility under canopy by cambering nose design and position rear seat ten inches higher than forward seat.

10. Designed fuel feed to include emergency manual cross-feed and allow all fuel to be sequenced to one engine. Also, provided for fuel to be gravity-fed to engines if fuel boost pumps should fail.

11. Provided special dual AC generator-supply power systems where if one fails, an automatic switchover cuts in and causes remaining generator to supply total load to aircraft.

12. Two identical hydraulic units, differing only in systems they supply, designed to be fully operated, along with the entire electrical and fuel systems, on only one engine.

These mandatory specifications had nothing to do with aircraft performance *per se*, but were meant to design out known sources of potential accidents. In 1956, for example, there were 197 major accidents caused by pilots who, for one reason or another, landed on concrete runways with the gear up. Part of the fault lay with inadequate gear-up warning systems and awkward placement of gear handles. Then there was the matter of a too-raucous warning horn installed on some aircraft to let the pilot know he was coming in with gear up. Probably apocryphal—but believable—is the story about a student testifying before an accident board as to why he came in gear up when mobile control was frantically screaming over the radio to lower gear. "I didn't hear the runway supervisor," the student is supposed to have said. "All that horn-blowing and those flares going up all over the runway distracted me."

The gear lever on the T-38 is easily reached with the left hand on the center console; three lights seen at the corner of his eye tell him if gear is down or up; and the warning horn can be cut off with a push of a finger.

The USAF T-38 Project Team took a good, hard look at the existing emergency fuel system problems that had brought too many T-33 and F-86 pilots to grief over the years. As originally installed, the emergency fuel switches

were located on the left vertical subpanels of both aircraft. Thus, at critical moments in flight, pilots had to drop
their heads and fumble for these lifesaving switches.
Eventually the switches were moved to the center panel
—where they belonged in the first place—but in the case
of the T-33 the emergency fuel switch was made to serve
three distinctly separate functions. The one switch was
used for airstart ignition, for emergency fuel, and to gang-
load the fuel pumps. All this on one switch. Blue-suits and
Northrop engineers went to work and came up with a
virtually goof-proof system. Boost pump switches with
protective covers fall easily to hand on the right subpanel
at about the height of the right knee, with the cross-feed
switch right in between.

Some Century fighters and later-model T-33s featured
radio channel selectors on the far right-hand side of the
cockpit. In making jet penetrations, pilots flying certain
models of these aircraft were last heard calling out that
they were changing channels. Diverting attention from
flight instruments to the inconveniently placed channel
selector resulted in disorientation under IFR conditions,
and unfortunate pilots simply augered in while in a high-
speed dive. So Northrop placed the channel selector in
the T-38 dead center at the top of the front pedestal,
directly beneath the attitude indicator and the TACAN.
With one sweep of his eyes the pilot can keep on instruments and still switch channels without upsetting his
orientation.

Two of the Century fighters feature all-important attitude gyros way over on the far left side of the instrument
console. This is no place for this instrument. On the T-38,
the MM-3 attitude gyro that tells the pilot whether he is
climbing or diving and how much he is banked to the

horizon is stuck at the very top of the center console. It is the most prominently placed instrument of them all; should the primary fail, there is a backup gyro installed just to the left and slightly below the big one.

In fact, the T-38 since its inception has been blessed with unusual cleanliness in its cockpit; "human engineering" has been carried out to a nearly idealized state of the art. The cockpits are roomy; even 200-lb. pilots wearing back-pack chutes don't have to be fitted in with shoehorns. There is elbow room and leg room. The interior is painted pale gray to give the impression of even more space and to soften harsh cast shadows thrown down at altitude.

Power plants chosen for the T-38 were J-85-5 axial flow eight-stage turbojets developing 2050 pounds of thrust each in MIL power, 2900 pounds each in MAX, or afterburner. These engines are not impressive in size, but they kick up a storm in performance. The J-85 weighs only 525 pounds, and delivers the highest thrust-to-weight ratio of any operational jet engine in the world. Grossed out with crew and 3790 pounds of fuel, the T-38 entire weighs only 11,760 pounds. (By comparison, the single-seat F-100C weighs fifteen tons.) For an airplane as cleanly configured as the T-38, less than six tons is not a whole lot of weight for nearly three tons of thrust to move at sea level. The T-38 accelerates from 0 to 100 knots (115 mph on the deck) within the first thousand feet of takeoff roll, and thereafter moves as though it had been catapulted into the sky. If you miss an approach, or come in too long, or are told to go around for any other reason, you move the throttle back into MIL and have what T-38 pilots fondly call "instant airspeed." You never have it with the big, heavy Centuries. The Talon's rate of climb at sea level is a phenomenal 30,800 feet per minute. It will climb 7,600 feet per minute on one engine alone. A stripped-down T-38 set a time-to-climb record in 1962 by topping 12,000 meters in 95.74 seconds, nearly 40,000 feet in just over a minute and a half. With reason, the T-38 is known to USAF pilots as the White Rocket.

For an airplane to pay handsome dividends to the Air Training Command it must not only be safe, but it must also have a quick turnaround time, and it must be easy to maintain. The quick turnaround is made possible by single-point refueling and a minimum of exterior check items prior to flight. The USAF-Northrop team made a study of the frequency of failures, where they occurred, and where most man-hours were spent in troubleshooting and maintenance in then-existing jet trainers. Components that seemed prone to give the most trouble were made easiest to get at for repair or replacement. A plug-in, plug-out concept was utilized wherever possible in order that a malfunctioning black-box of electronics that needed over-haul would not ground the whole airplane. About 25 per-cent of the fuselage area is devoted to various access panels so that troubleshooting—most of it at eye level—is made as painless as possible.

Engine-driven accessories were mounted in the airframe instead of the engine to provide maximum accessibility. Integrated power packages for each engine—AC generator, gear box, and hydraulic pump—were mounted below and forward of the engines. One or both power packages can be removed through access doors without having to get at the engines themselves. Conversely, engines can be pulled out of the rear of the airplane without having to remove the power packages. Engines are mounted on an

overhead track and roller arrangement fixed to the airframe; pulling one engine out and installing another can be done by a competent crew within less than thirty minutes.

Outside of the fact that the USAF-Northrop team produced a beautiful aircraft with impressive performance, the unprecedented cooperation between civilian and military resulted in a bonus achievement: the T-38 won the distinction of being the first supersonic jet aircraft to complete its entire research and development program without a single flight accident. This was good news indeed, but a few skeptics pointed out that the R & D phase was conducted by skilled test pilots who had a great fund of aerodynamic and engineering knowledge. Would your average student pilot with only 120 hours of T-37 time be able to cope with a sensitive supersonic aircraft with high sink rate characteristics? USAF determined to find out. ATC culled twenty-six students from Class 62-F scattered among several training bases, seeking an average group in order to get a fair judgment of the student–T-38 mating. These twenty-six gathered at Randolph tagged Class 62-FZ, and training began. Twenty-five students graduated—an astonishing lack of attrition—and there were no accidents, not even a blown tire. From an original forty T-38s ordered by ATC, the figure was jumped and jumped again until today there are more than seven hundred Talons on operational training duty with the Air Force.

"O.K., let's kick the tire and light the fire." Major Donald L. Elwood was having a little joke with his student, Second Lieutenant Dennis M. Ridnover of Knoxville, Iowa. What Ridnover's IP meant was that they were going to preflight the airplane before Ridnover's maiden trip aloft in a T-38. With the fat yellow checklist in his hand, Ridnover followed the Major through the ritual.

The Form 781 was checked to note the status and prior servicing of the plane; the crew chief had passed along no discrepancies. Seat and canopy pins were seen to be installed, and the right navigational publications were aboard. Stuffing the 781 back in the cockpit, Elwood led Ridnover on a circuit of the entire airplane, beginning with the left forward section. They checked the intake duct, the cabin pressurization static port, the wheel well, removal of gear safety pin, the tire, the Pitot tube, and static vents. Skirting the Pitot boom, they paralleled the right forward section, ticking off the right cabin pressurization port, level of the brake reservoir, and the intake duct. Dipping underneath the sharp-edged wing, they gave their attention to the speed brake well, the wheel well, removal of the gear safety pin, extension of the strut, the tire, and the wing itself. Then at the right aft section they noted that the hydraulic fluid level was up and that the underside of the fuselage showed no signs of hydraulic or oil leaks. Back at the tail section they ran their eyes over the empennage and poked their heads into the tailpipes to make sure there were no dents, cracks, or leaking fuel. They checked the hydraulic fluid level on the left side of the fuselage. This is a circular, glassed-over level indicator that can be checked in flight by a pilot in another aircraft, if he flies very close to the airplane which seems to be losing hydraulic fluid. Continuing to the left center section, they repeated the check performed on the opposite center section—wing, tire, strut, gear pin, wheel and speed brake wells.

All this is the "kick the tire" part of T-38 exterior in-

spection. Now Elwood and Ridnover were ready to climb inside the cockpits and prepare to light the fire.

Each fastened and adjusted seat belt, shoulder harness, seat belt lanyard, zero lanyard, oxygen connectors, hose retention strap and helmet chin strap. They checked to be sure the ejection handgrips were in the full down position and each ran through the PRICE oxygen check. Elwood flicked the battery switch to ON, bringing the radios to life. He ran quickly through the left console check: gear door switch, NORMAL; flight director system shutoff switch, ON; rudder trim knob, CENTERED; wing flap lever, OFF, speed brake switch, OPEN, and throttles, OFF. Then he checked that the landing gear lever was down, switched the compass to MAG, made sure the fuel cutoff switches were set at NORMAL and that the landing light switch was OFF. The accelerometer, cabin altimeter, and airspeed indicator were checked. The clock was set. The steering and navigation mode switches were set, and the marker beacon light was tested. Radio transfer and intercom switches were clicked into place, and rows of black circuit-breaker buttons were inspected to make sure none had popped up. Barometric pressure reading came in through the headphones from the tower, and the altimeter was set. The vertical velocity indicated that the silent T-38 was neither climbing nor diving, so that was all right. The cabin air switch was set to PRESS., the Pitot heat switch to OFF, the magnetic compass was checked, the fuel boost pump switches were turned to ON, the cross-feed switch to ON, and the generator switches to ON. Fuel and oxygen quantities were checked, and the warning-light test switch was checked. That came on, the gear-down warning horn blew, and now they were ready to start engines.

Power to ground-start the engines is provided by a small turbojet engine known as a palouste, housed inside a large yellow cab on wheels. The palouste delivers about 400 pounds of exhaust, which is force-fed into the second-stage turbines of the T-38 engines via a long flex hose. The pilot twirls a gloved finger over his helmet as a signal to start the air supply. Then he stabs a finger against the right engine start button. This automatically positions a diverter valve which directs the blast of hot air against the right turbine buckets. As they begin to spin and whine, the pilot eases the right throttle around the horn to IDLE, which energizes the ignition exciters and fires main and afterburner sparking plugs, while starting metered fuel flow into the combustion chamber ("burner cans"). This spray of fuel mixed with air rushes past the hot spark with a resulting controlled explosion that kicks a tornado of exhaust gases out of the tailpipe at 100 mph with a temperature of nearly 500 degrees Fahrenheit. The pilot checks his EGT gauge, engine rpm at idle (not less than 12 percent), and oil pressure. With these needles in the green, the starting procedure is repeated for the left engine. The airplane is disconnected from its palouste umbilical and is on its own internal power, ready for taxi and flight.

The exciting difference between the Tweet and the T-38 is felt by the new student pilot the instant the IP moves the throttles into MAX, firing the afterburners. Fifty-eight hundred pounds of thrust kicks you in the rump—a cannonading reminder of the power now at your disposal. Boots come off the brakes just prior to AB initiation, and right away you experience the sudden acceleration of the Talon's famous six-mile-per-minute climb capability. The airspeed needle swings quickly to 140 knots, the stick is moved back, rotating the aircraft to takeoff attitude, and a few seconds and fifteen knots later you simply fly off the ground—airborne after a ground roll the length of seven football fields.

On the climb to altitude the IP keeps up a stream of well-rehearsed chatter delivered in a monotone. Stay alert. Swivel your head, especially on climbout. Watch out for formation of birds. A student and his IP punched out of their T-38 last week over Utah on a cross-country out of Reese. Feathered flak made a mess out of both engines. Guys got down okay, but the plane was a write-off. Watch out for other aircraft, too. Give some attention to the EGTs, fuel flow and fuel quantity readings, rpm, and oil pressure. We're through ten thousand feet; disconnect zero lanyard and clip it to the stowage ring. Check blinker and oxygen supply. Keep your visor down. If we had to bail out of this thing fast, it could save your life.

Before the realization has time to sink in that he is moving faster than he has moved before, the student feels the airplane verge toward zero G, then settle smoothly as the plane comes out over the top at 45,000 feet, or, as he will write it later, at FL 450. Nine miles high over Texas. Smooth as nylon. No birds up here; they would all be fatally hypoxic even if they had the lift to get here. It is strange to sit way up front here by yourself, after all those weeks working elbow-to-elbow with the IP stuffed in beside you. The IP is some distance to the rear, walled in. He's elevated and can see me; but all I can see of him through the canted Plexiglas screen is part of his white helmet, a reflection of the sun on the dark-brown visor, and part of the green rubber snout that keeps him breath-

ing. We share the same oxygen, the same intercom
channel, the same sensations of flight . . . but that's about
all. Because the rear-view mirror is convex, he looks
smaller and farther away still. But his voice is loud and
clear in my earphones, and he'll catch every tiny goof I
make in the months we will spend together in this airplane.

The orientation ride is a non-graded flight lasting one
short hour. The student is shown the restricted areas, the
auxiliary field, the boundaries of the high and low areas
where the T-38 is allowed to operate with and without
positive (radar) control from the ground. Then the IP
demonstrates a small sampling of the T-38's pleasurable
flying qualities. He kicks in the burners and slides them
through the Mach, then lets the student try it—an effort-
less, heady accomplishment that will inspire a letter
written that same evening which begins: "Dear Mom/
Dad/Mary Lou: Today I went supersonic!"

Then, at about 400 knots indicated, the IP enters a
shallow pitched up 20 degrees. He eases off back pressure
and slowly applies full rudder. The T-38 rolls through
the sky without any help from the ailerons. The IP explains that other sweptwing aircraft have this same capability, and that it's a good thing to know about if you ever
face a split-flap situation or suffer structural damage and
can't bring the wings level with aileron alone.

Okay, the IP says, this bear is fast and she's sensitive
to control—especially at high Mach or in turbulence.
You've got to avoid rapid deceleration at high Mach at
low altitude. Coming off the power abruptly under those
conditions of flight can produce transverse G forces that
can push the pilot forward into the stick. These precau-
tions take nothing away from the T-38's inherent stability,

easily demonstrable. With the rudder-limiter engaged to prevent the rudder from swiveling more than six degrees on either side of the axis, and with the wings level, the IP slowly applies full rudder and releases abruptly. The T-38 slides, then begins gentle oscillations about the yaw axis. After four or five periods of oscillation, the T-38 dampens out and resumes a normal flight attitude. There is more. One of the black boxes up in the nose controls the T-38's Stability Augmenter System, a device consisting of an electronic components assembly, a yaw rate gyro, and a yaw electrohydraulic servo actuator. This system automatically senses and dampens short-period yaw os-cillations. With the SAS switched on, the IP again gives it full rudder and releases. As before, the airplane yaws, but the SAS takes hold and returns the T-38 to yaw-free flight after only a period and a half of oscillation. The student gets the right idea: the T-38 flies "hands off" when treated gently and with respect.

After practicing with the fuel cross-feed system and a demonstration of how the speed brakes can double the rate of descent without getting on the power or dropping the nose too steeply, the plane heads for the barn. Enter the traffic pattern at 280 KIAS; pitchout for turn on down-wind leg and gear down at 240 knots or less; 100-percent flaps before turn to base leg; pitchout for turn onto final at 175 knots plus one knot for every hundred pounds of fuel remaining over one thousand pounds; final approach at 155 knots plus fuel, then touch down at 130 knots plus fuel, rotate for maximum aerodynamic braking, and let the nosewheel make contact with the runway. This first flight in a T-38 is the shortest sixty minutes of air time the student will ever know; it is his introduction to the new

Twenty-five hours of judo provide pilots with a margin of survival if shot down over the jungles of Southeast Asia.

world of supersonic flight, a presentation of the ultimate challenge offered by Air Training Command.

Better to enable student pilots to cope with the T-38 under all conditions of flight, a radical change was recently made in the curriculum. Students are taught to fly instruments early in the program instead of learning IFR after all of the contact lessons have been successfully passed. After the first orientation ride in the Talon, the student spends the next eleven hours of flight in a blind world, under a canvas hood alone with the glittering array of control, performance, and navigation instruments. The only time during the instrument flight missions the student has any visual references to the outside world is during entry to the traffic pattern and landing. Otherwise, he is alone with the needles and the numerals to show him where he is and where he is going.

Before the instruments-first theory was formulated, tested, and finally included in the syllabus, almost the total knowledge of contact flying required of a student prior to first solo was crammed into the first three and one-half weeks of T-38 instruction. There was simply too much to be learned. There were other problems. When the pilot production rate doubled over the preceding few years, airspace grew less and less; the sky became dangerously crowded. Contact missions were forced into the area of positive control, above 24,000 feet, where instrument flight rules prevailed. Students were having trouble with traffic patterns and landings. The T-38 comes in hot and high-pitched, and the wings are so far back they are useless aids to composite flying—you can't see the tips to line them up on the horizon as a check for zero bank. To see if students with a thorough grounding in instrument flight could more easily get through first solo and beyond, experimental classes at Williams AFB in Arizona and at Vance AFB in Oklahoma were taught using the instruments-first syllabus. Results showed that transition from T-37 to T-38 was easier and that later contact missions were flown more successfully, with fewer problems in the areas of traffic entry and landings. Instrument approaches to landing, including ground-controlled approaches by radar, closely approximate airspeeds, attitudes, configurations, and "feel" necessary for flying contact or visual approaches. All this practice was a bonus to the student when the initial instrument phase was completed and he reverted to contact flying again. The student then, as now, solos sometime after the sixth week of T-38 training instead of before the fourth week. He brings to first solo a higher level of flight experience and greater confidence than ever before.

The instrument-first student finds that this training is also a form of free life insurance. If he's caught upstairs on a solo contact mission that becomes an IFR situation because of sudden weather, or if his home field is closed, he is able to fly an actual weather penetration or radar approach if necessary. Not all experiments conducted with the training syllabus are successful, but teaching them to fly instruments first has been outstandingly so. It makes better, safer pilots. Of the total of 120 hours of flight in the T-38, nearly thirty hours are spent on instruments, leaving thirty-five hours for contact missions (three hours are spent on night flying), eighteen hours for navigation flights, and thirty-four hours of formation work. All of these missions require constant use of combinations of any of the twenty-one instruments that stud the front panel.

One significant example of how control and performance instruments are used in conjunction with TACAN
and ground radar to get a T-38 pilot home safely under
adverse weather conditions can be shown by re-creating
a flight that finds a Talon having to let down through
clouds and overcast, flying in a soupy, opaque world until
almost the moment of touchdown.

TACAN is a short-range navigation system that supplies
continuous slant-range distance and bearing information
presented on the HSI (Horizontal Situation Indicator)
located in the center of the panel, just underneath the
attitude indicator. The ground part of the TACAN system
consists of a transponder and a rotating antenna for transmission to the HSI in the airplane. Slant-range distance to
the TACAN station is read off from the DME (Distance
Measuring Equipment) window, a cut-out which reveals
numerals revolving on a drum. These numerals tell the
pilot how far he is in nautical miles from the selected
station. Accuracy of the DME is high, within plus or minus
600 feet, plus two-tenths of one percent of the distance
being measured. At a distance of ten miles, the error will
exceed no more than plus or minus 720 feet. The main
dial of the HSI shows the bearing of the station in degrees,
and by keeping a miniature aircraft on the dial centered
on a movable bar the pilot can stay dead on course. If
the flight path shifts left or right, the movable bar instantly
tells him how much course deviation must be corrected for.

On the initial approach to Laughlin, the pilot will be
monitoring several instruments, cross-checking from one
to the other; his whole attention will not be riveted to the
HSI. He must watch his vertical velocity indicator to
make sure the rate of descent is as planned, the airspeed
indicators and tachometers to see that he is holding ap-

proximately 90-percent power and 250 KIAS, altimeter and attitude indicator. And he will scan the EGT gauges, fuel flow, fuel quantity, oil and hydraulic pressure dials. At nine miles out, the T-38 is picked up by the surveillance radar and then is switched to a more refined system for a precision radar letdown. From this point on, the whole procedure is dependent upon voice communications between controller and pilot, who receives a current altimeter setting and report of what the weather is like on the deck. The pilot of Air Force T-38 Jet Number 38159 now begins his terse communications with the controller, a highly trained Airman sitting before his scanners inside the mobile radar van parked by the side of the runway.

Controller: Five niner, this is a precision approach to runway 13L, continue heading two five zero, descend to one thousand five hundred feet.

Pilot: Five niner, Roger. Two five zero, one thousand five hundred feet.

Controller: Five niner, landing is on runway one three left, one five zero feet wide, eight thousand six hundred feet long, field elevation is one zero eight one feet.

Pilot: Five niner, Roger.

Controller: Five niner, make all turns standard rate.

Pilot: Five niner.

Controller: Five niner, you are six miles northwest on downwind leg. Perform landing cockpit check.

Pilot: Five niner.

Controller: Five niner, range eight miles northwest, turn left heading zero eight zero, maintain one thousand five hundred feet for base leg.

Pilot: Five niner, Roger. Zero eight zero, one thousand five hundred feet.

Controller: Five niner, range eight miles on base leg. Check gear down, stand by for turn to final.

Pilot: Five niner, Roger.
Controller: Five niner, turn left heading one five zero. Main-
                    tain one thousand five hundred feet for final
                    approach.
Pilot: Five niner, Roger. One five zero, one thousand
                    five hundred feet.
Controller: Five niner, range seven miles on final. Switch to
                    channel niner one for final controller.
Pilot: Five niner, Roger.
Controller: Five niner, this is Laughlin radar final controller.
                    How do you read me?
Pilot: Five niner, loud and clear.
Controller: Five niner, now on final approach. Do not ac-
                    knowledge further transmissions. Make final flap
                    setting prior to intercepting glide path. Check
                    gear down. Now five miles from touchdown
                    approaching glide path. Begin descent at six
                    hundred feet per minute. Heading is one one
                    five. On glide path. Range four miles from touch-
                    down. Twenty-five feet above glide path, adjust
                    your rate of descent. On course, heading one
                    one five. Cleared to land. Three miles from
                    touchdown, now fifteen feet above glide path.
                    Now on glide path. On course, two and a half
                    miles from touchdown. Going ten feet below
                    glide path, adjust your rate of descent. Range
                    now, two miles from touchdown. Now on glide
                    path, heading one one five. Range one and a half
                    miles from touchdown, on course, on glide path.
                    Precision minimums. One mile from touchdown.
                    On course, on glide path. Over end of runway.
                    Approaching touchdown. On course, on glide
                    path. Over touchdown point now, cleared to
                    tower frequency. Out.

During an approach such as this one—and they are
routine—the pilot is frantically busy with his eyes, calm
with his hands. He watches the magnetic compass, re-

ligiously holding a precise heading. He flicks his attention back and forth from the vertical velocity indicator to the attitude indicator, holding a steady 600 fpm descent with wings level. The slightest deviations from heading or rate of descent are made with tentative touches to rudder and aileron controls. He stays glued to the gauges, and he does *not* look up to see what may be going on outside the confines of the cockpit; to do so means to risk instant spatial disorientation with probable fatal results, that close to the ground. By the time he is over the end of the runway, shadows may suddenly appear in the cockpit, and he knows he is now in the clear, that the familiar concrete ribbon is plainly visible. Then he can shift his attention away from the panel and execute a normal landing while the controller's voice still crackles in his ears, the voice of some Sergeant or Airman who would blush if you told him pilots look upon RAPCON controllers as some sort of guardian angels whose dry metallic tones are sweeter than music. Especially under IFR.

Most T-38 students solo the White Rocket after twenty-five hours of dual, including the eleven hours of instrument flight that precedes a solid block of contact flying that puts the student on his mettle as far as acrobatics and landing stages are concerned. Acro in the T-38 is done precisely the same way acro is done in the T-37, except that it is done at much higher Mach numbers and under greater G loads. One husky youngster just down from the High Area, where he bathed himself in honest sweat after wringing out his T-38, sipped coffee from a heavy mug, lost in thought. "Thing that gets me," he said finally, "is that they *pay* us for this."

The four hours of formation flying in the T-37 become

thirty-four in the T-38, every hour of which is preparation for the exacting demands that will be imposed on the pilot when he graduates and is sent to a TAC combat training wing, where they tuck it in tight—and woe to the wingman who cannot stay wired to his leader. Formation flying is exhilarating; no more exciting game of follow the leader has been devised. You close in on the leader from left and behind and line up the leading edge of his wingtip with the center of the star painted on his fuselage. Then, in proper "fingertip" formation with your wingtip no farther than three feet from his, you follow him through the sky at 500 mph, seven miles above the earth. When he pulls a 3G turn, you turn with him, never losing the wingtip-to-wingtip alignment. You must watch not only the close relationship between his airplane and yours, but for his hand signals—there is almost no radio chatter in formation work. If he signals for a cross-under from left wing to right you have to be ready to respond immediately, moving throttle and controls gently, gently, gently. Pull off power, compensate with a touch of stick aft, dropping a few feet lower than standard fingertip. Hold off power until your nose clears his tail, then nudge the throttle forward to maintain nose-to-tail spacing. Then slight aileron pressure to begin sliding over on the other side with a slight change of heading. You watch his blackened tailpipes spewing heat as they slide across to your left, then you come level again with aileron until your left wingtip is resting three feet off his right. A touch of aileron coordinated with rudder brings you back on the leader's heading, and if all has been done with finesse you should see his right wingtip planted squarely in the center of the star. This never happens the first time, of course, and it is only with hours of practice that a cross-under can be done all in one smooth movement.

On rare occasions, as much fancy footwork is required on the ground as it is in the air. Two-ship formation takeoffs are always exciting to watch, sometimes more so than others. A pair of T-38s had just completed engine run-up, and everything was in the green. Lead came off the brakes and moved the throttles into MAX. However, the right afterburner lit first, and the unequal thrust caused a sharp yaw to the left. The student, alert to what had happened, applied heavy right rudder to compensate —at which moment the left burner lighted off with its usual peal of thunder. The student hastily applied full left rudder, and the airplane yawed left. The IP shouted "I've got it!" and went to work with his feet on the rudders while pulling off power to IDLE. Right rudder, for some unfathomable reason, seemed to be taking the airplane off the runway, so he pumped in some left.

Meanwhile, the IP flying wing was watching lead's strange behavior, trying to figure out what lead was trying to do. Was he aborting the takeoff? If so, he must decide —quickly—whether to abort along with the leader or to get his own airplane off the ground in AB and thus leave the entire runway clear for lead to straighten out his directional difficulties. Fortunately—as it turned out—the student in the Number Two ship had come off the brakes a second late, which placed the airplane a half-ship length behind lead at the start of takeoff roll. The decision as to whether to abort or continue takeoff was taken out of the IP's hands when lead began to swerve left, directly into the path of the onrushing Number Two. He was 90 degrees to his path, and the danger of colliding with the other

$600,000 airplane was great. The IP yanked the throttle back to IDLE while at the same time coming down hard with his boots on the brakes. The sudden deceleration swung the airplane around in a complete 360-degree turn; it came off the runway, back on again, and came to a quick stop with the left main gear in the grass.

While Number Two was doing its three-sixty, so was lead, which finally was brought to a halt 1500 feet down the runway from where the takeoff roll had begun. All four main gear tires were a smoking mess and had to be replaced, but no other damage was done. Instinctive reaction on the part of the IPs saved the airplanes, not to mention the men inside them. Maintenance people quickly found the culprit: the nosewheel steering button in the lead T-38 was stuck in the ON position at the critical moment of brakes-off.

Incidents such as these inevitably lead to the question, Is military flying dangerous? The danger lies in the potential, not in the fact. A low-time student at the controls of a high-performance, mechanically complex aircraft flying through crowded airspace at speeds ranging from 250 knots to supersonic sets up a potentially dangerous situation. Yet, the accident rate in Air Training Command runs at a rate of 2.5 major accidents per 100,000 flying hours. "Major accident" does not mean a fatal crash; by definition, a major is one that "bends the bird" badly enough to require appreciable maintenance. A jet that overshoots a landing, loses its brakes, and plows into the runway barrier, wiping out the gear and denting the nose, is classed as a major accident, even if the pilot walks away unhurt. By comparison, the overall USAF accident rate (all commands) runs at 4.6 per 100,000 hours. In short,

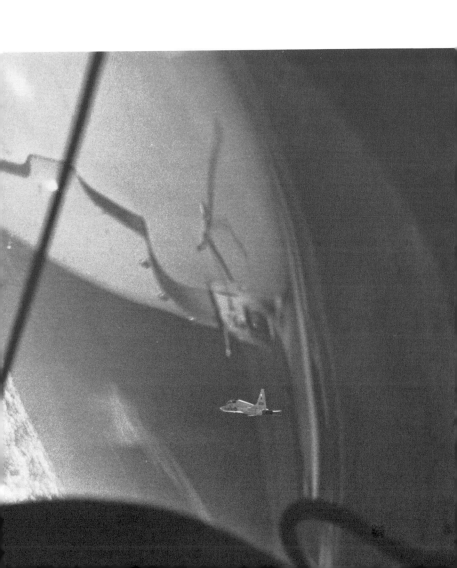

today's training process has been made safer than all other kinds of flying combined. During World War II, it was just the opposite.

There are good reasons for this. Most ATC flying is done in daylight, under Visual Flight Rules. The terrain surrounding ATC bases poses few dangers, i.e., there are no high mountains in Texas, Oklahoma, southern parts of Georgia and Alabama, or in lower Arizona. Very seldom does weather become a danger factor in any of these states, and when it does, "instrument-first" students and sophisticated navigation gear enable planes to be guided home. The training aircraft, with two engines, are more reliable than before. The quality and depth of instruction are superior, and students are more mature and better educated when they enter the UPT program than were their fathers and older brothers. The entire flight-training program is rigidly standardized; there is never any doubt about procedures under any given danger situation. As we have seen earlier, students are well drilled in survival techniques in case dire emergency faces them in the air. Improved ejection seats and automatic parachutes give pilots every chance to escape disabled aircraft in flight.

If American automobile drivers were as carefully screened as military pilots, if they were as strenuously educated, if they were washed out for ineptitude, and if they were given the right kind of automobiles for U.S. traffic situations, then the situation would improve drastically. But the fact remains that, mile for mile, you are *six times safer* flying in military jet aircraft than you are driving cars on American highways and city streets.

When graduation time rolls around, the student closes

his logbook with 240 hard-earned hours. Stored in his head is the important residue of another 920 hours spent in classrooms and on athletic fields. Drawn up in ranks, he receives the fruit of his labors: those coveted silver wings pinned to his blouse, where they will be glanced at out of the corner of his eye twenty or thirty times a day for many days to come, and a large pale-blue certificate proclaiming the fact that the recipient is (finally!) a Military Pilot.

It is an end, and a beginning.

CHAPTER 10

SCHOOL FOR COMBAT

It is still pitch black, and cold, when the first engine explodes into life. You know right away that no training airplane can make that amount of noise, which can come only from a bird of war. The windows of your room shake in their leaded frames from the shock waves, and you are—or were—asleep inside a concrete building a full half-mile from the line. It's still early for first takeoff, and the night refueling mission went to bed two hours ago, so the racket is coming from a J75 some crew chief is running up to the satisfaction of his ear and the gauges. For maybe ten seconds the awesome thunder reverberates throughout the room, subsides, then dies out altogether. Once jerked instantly from sleep by the urgent firing of an F-105 means staying alert for the rest of the day. You give yourself sixty seconds, then throw off the covers and trot across the carpet and onto the cold tile of the shower, turning handles to get the stinging needles of warm water going. Dressed in thermal long johns, flight suit, jacket, warm socks, and boots, you clatter down the metal steps of the fire escape and head for the club. The stars are fading in a suddenly pale sky. You walk faster, anticipating the eggs and the sausage and, above all, the cups of steaming coffee. Eight miles to the northeast, the pleasure palaces of the Las Vegas Strip have slowed for respite. Casinos, like vampires, are not compatible with the threat of a rising sun.

Fighter pilot! There is still meaning and magic in that phrase—especially to a select breed of men living in a nation at war. Nearly eighty percent of UPT graduates dream of strapping themselves to a twenty-ton, Mach 2-plus combat airplane when they have made their last

172

ride in T-38s. There are two direct routes to active par-
ticipation as a fighter jock in the air war over the out-
country of North Vietnam. One is to sweat out the back
seat of an F4-C for an indeterminate period of time as a
co-pilot-in-tandem, letting the guy up front do most of
the flying. The other, preferred, plum is to transition directly into a single-seat F-105D, the airplane that has
carried out seventy-five percent of the tactical and strategic bombing strikes against targets north of the DMZ.
Republic's F-105, variously referred to by pilots as "Thud,"
"Squash Bomber," and "Lead Sled," was originally designed as a low-level city buster. Equipped with fantastic
radar and navigation devices, the Thud's mission was to
roar in fifty to one hundred feet off the deck, zoom up
and toss-bomb a nuke, then light off the AB, and sprint
away from the impending destruction far faster than the
speed of sound. Nearly 900 F-105s of various models were
manufactured before the production lines closed down.
For years, many believed the F-105 was a mistake; electronic maintenance was an absolute nightmare, and it
seemed that more Fives were in the shop at any one time
than could be put into the air. However, the bugs were
pinched out one by one, and the Thud is now recognized
as the outstanding fighter-bomber of the Vietnam war.
Like most sweptwing, high sink-rate, high wing-load aircraft, the Thud is not a happy airplane to fly at slow speeds
near the deck—but when pushed to 500 knots and above,
the Five handles like a thoroughbred.

The recent UPT graduate, upon first introduction to the
F-105, cannot help being awed; the Five is *huge*. The fuselage is sixty-four feet, five inches long. From the ground
to the top of the tailfin is nearly twenty feet. The wings,

placed on the "shoulder" of the bullet-like fuselage, span
thirty-four feet, eleven inches. And the engine: the Pratt &
Whitney J75-P-19W is a monster that in afterburner with
water-injection delivers 26,500 pounds of thrust, which is
three times the thrust available from *both* engines on the
T-38. In clean configuration above 35,000 feet the F-105D
will hit Mach 2.1. The Thud is incredibly strong; subsonic,
the plane can withstand 8.67 positive Gs and 3 negative
Gs before airframe integrity is threatened, and supersonic
it can handle nearly the same G forces. Whereas the T-38
can get airborne with a max gross weight of just under
12,000 pounds, the F-105 can, on a cool day, lift off with a
max gross of 52,800 pounds. This is one airplane pilots
fresh from Air Training Command must confront and
master in order to become bona fide fighter jocks. Seventy-
nine sorties in the F-105 and they are ready for combat.

Combat. That word is the sole reason for existence of the
new Tactical Fighter Weapons Center at Nellis AFB in
Nevada. It is here that pilot skills are honed for delivery
of ordnance in support of tactical or strategic objectives,
where men are taught to attain and hold air superiority
against the principal enemy: Russian-built MIGs flown by
whoever flies them, over whatever terrain the Communists
choose to wage war. The Center is a two-wing organiza-
tion, one charged with crew training, the other serving as
an IP school and as an advanced laboratory for tactical
procedures as applied to the war in Vietnam and whatever
war we may become involved in later. The whole is commanded by Brigadier General Ralph G. Taylor, Jr., who
does not command other fighter jocks by virtue of rank
alone; during World War II he shot down four Me 109s

and a brace of Macchi 202s as a fighter pilot in the ETO.

Nellis is a Valhalla for the living. More experienced air warriors are here than anywhere else in the world—except in Southeast Asia. Fighter pilots abound, from all recent wars and with experience in every theater. Lieutenant Colonel Fred A. Treyz is a good example.

"Fritz the Fox" is CO of the 26th Squadron, one of three squadrons that make up the 4520th Combat Crew Training Wing. There is no mistaking a pilot of the 26th. On his right shoulder he wears the red and blue patch of a striking cobra, symbol of an attitude and of a unit spirit. The Fox has commanded the 26th Cobras since 1965, but like every other rated fighter pilot his request for combat duty in SEA will inevitably be honored, and Colonel Treyz will once again assume his natural role of leading other men against the enemy.

The route the Fox has taken to the cockpit of a Century fighter has been circuitous, but never lacking in heading. Treyz graduated from a high school in Middleton, N.Y., and jumped immediately into the USAAF cadet program in November 1942. He became qualified on P-51 Mustangs and P-38 Lightnings and was ordered to the Pacific Theater with an operational squadron at the tail end of the war. Two years of hard training went begging; when the war ended, Treyz had never fired a shot, and he quickly learned that fighter pilots were a surplus item in the national inventory. To deny a born aviator the right to fly is to deny him soul. Using savings and severance pay, Treyz bought an aging Stearman biplane for six hundred dollars, spent twice that amount for a new engine, then set himself up in business as a crop duster in Arizona. Pickings were as lean as the work was dangerous, and Treyz re-

Fritz the Fox.

Unbuttoned, the F-105 displays electronic innards that enable the Thud to virtually fly itself to any target in the world.

Gatling guns spewing 20-mm. rounds from six rotating barrels are harmonized to produce tight groups at killing range.

sorted to clever ruses in order to feed his wife and child. Dressed in white cap and overalls and carrying large brushes, he passed himself off as a non-union painter and contracted for entire houses, learning how to paint as he went along. A sudden hangar fire reduced his Stearman to non-insured ashes one night, leaving Treyz little more than his brushes and an undiminished faith in his own future in American aviation.

Hungry days followed, until Treyz was taken on as a pilot with Frontier Airlines. At last he was back in the air, but hauling passengers from one point to another was not his idea of thrilling flight. It only helped pay the bills. Jets from Williams and Luke filled the Arizona sky, their thunder seeming to mock the fighter-trained pilot who plowed through the air at one-fifty indicated. Then the Korean War started, and Treyz was called back into uniform to transition into B-29s. He flew combat missions against strategic targets north of the 38th Parallel until Personnel gave in to his repeated requests for transfer and shipped him off to learn to fly F-84G "Hogs," a plane Treyz flew in war and in peace without incident until one day in 1956 when his Hog exploded in the air 20,000 feet over the city of Ponce, Puerto Rico. The explosion blew the tail section completely off the fuselage, and Treyz punched out. He drifted in a silent sky for twenty-one minutes, then splashed into the warm waters of the Caribbean. He ducked out of the chute and swam only a few strokes until his boots scraped sand. He walked ashore upright, wet but unhurt. Treyz's jet career continued with a tour on F-102 delta-winged interceptors, then with the 36th TAC Fighter Wing flying F-105s out of Bitburg, Germany. Treyz is proof that once a fighter pilot, always a fighter pilot.

The Cobras' Operations Officer is another old pro, Lieutenant Colonel James H. Caldwell, sometime of Charleston, Mississippi. Jim Caldwell joined the USAAF cadet program late in 1944, but like thousands of others at that stage of the war was kept around doing useless jobs such as painting rocks and flagpoles and never got inside an airplane. He went on to graduate from the Naval Academy at Annapolis in 1950, elected to take his commission from the Air Force, and went to combat in Korea with the 58th TAC Fighter Wing. Caldwell completed his hundred missions and was never hit. He has been flying Thuds since 1962 and did a pair of split tours in Southeast Asia, flying F-105s out of Thailand to bomb and strafe targets in the North. During the time Jim Caldwell spent in combat he lost ten close friends out of his squadron to enemy ground fire, but he always managed to bring his Thud back home to Takhli, sometimes punctured with Chinese-made rifle and machine-gun bullets. Caldwell fully expects to be sent back into combat after a tour Stateside. In the meantime, his job is to help train others in the demanding art of laying down ordnance with precision.

The new student is quick to discover that the F-105 is not just an airplane; it is a weapons system capable of hurting the enemy in a multitude of ways. If world politics degenerate to the point of committing Ultimate War, a single F-105 hung with fuel and carrying a nuke inside the bomb bay can dash faster than the speed of sound at altitudes too low for radar detection and smash an entire city more effectively than whole wings of B-17s were able to do yesteryear. When a switch is turned to AUTOSS, the Thud will fly itself to the target, pull itself up in a steep climb, automatically toss the bomb, then roll itself over straight and level for a fast getaway. There are also

four other ways in which a pilot can deliver a nuke out
of AUTOSS mode, including the VLADD system. Visual
Low Angle Drogue Delivery means that the pilot flies the
airplane manually, but electronics works for him to indicate precisely when to initiate delivery. He chooses a
target reference point near the target and at a known distance from planned center of impact. When the airplane
is over the reference point, he activates timers with the
freeze-fire button. The timers flash the hi-toss/pull-up
light when the aircraft is at the right distance from the
target. Upon this visual signal the pilot goes into full MIL
power and begins a wings-level pull-up so as to obtain
4 Gs within 3.5 seconds. At a pitch angle of 40 degrees he
comes off the Gs and enters a straightaway climb. It is
just before this point that the bomb will go, descending
to earth under a drogue chute. Practicing delivery of nukes
takes up only four of the 124 hours of sortie time available
—but those four hours are enough to enable any one F-105
pilot to scrape away a target city on either side of the
Urals.

Priority in training missions is given to tactics that will
be applied directly to the war in Vietnam. The widely
scattered gunnery ranges that dot the three-million-acre
shooting gallery that is Nellis are laid out with dummy
targets just as the pilots will find them when they go into
combat. SAM sites are built in the familiar Star of David
patterns the Vietcong use. Simulated petroleum stores are
revetted in typical North Vietnamese fashion, built to scale
and located near airstrips bulldozed on the desert floor.
These realistic targets are bombed, strafed, smeared with
napalm, and pocked with strikes from air-launched rockets
delivered from low altitudes and at high speeds. Only

jungle terrain and curtains of flak are missing from this training ground for war in Asia.

The tactical formation taught all American fighter pilots is a basic four-ship spread known as the "fluid four." The leader of the first two-ship element is high man, staying from 500 to 2000 feet above ground level in undefended areas, and upwards of 6000 feet over areas of known flak concentrations. His wingman, Number Two in the flight, stays about 2000 feet back at a 45-degree angle to the leader's plane, and anywhere from 500 to 2000 feet below. Leader of the second element, Number Three man, maintains approximately 5000 feet separation from Number One, and his wingman, Number Four, is positioned at the same relative angle as Number Two. Thus the formation resembles somewhat a thumbless hand with fingers outstretched. Indeed, the forerunner of the fluid four was employed by the Luftwaffe during World War II and was then adopted by the RAF, who called it "finger four."

The formation, standard in all TAC units, provides maximum flexibility and is especially suited for armed reconnaissance, or search-and-destroy, missions. The leader is constantly changing his heading, altitude, and airspeed as the flight progresses, which gives the enemy headaches in trying to lay his guns. The formation itself provides maximum sweep area for eyeball observation of the terrain below and leaves no blind spots to the rear where MIGs could sneak in undetected. Since each airplane is at a different height, the angle of observation of each pilot varies from vertical to near-horizontal, so the Vietcong irregulars and the regular North Vietnam Army are forced to camouflage their equipment on all sides, not just on the top. Because the lead element is so far out ahead of the other

Cliver briefs for morning strike. This month, Nevada; next month, Asia.

element, there is time for the second element to make a
follow-up attack upon a target of opportunity spotted and
clobbered by the leader and his wingman. Not the least
consideration of the fluid-four formation is the fact that
each element can handily support the other if bounced by
enemy jets.

Ground attack and armed recce missions are flown more
than any other type at the Center. These training sorties
are planned and led by students like First Lieutenant Jeff
Cliver, of Mt. Holly, New Jersey. Cliver stands six-feet-
two, has the build of a long-distance runner, blue eyes,
and a shock of yellow hair. Cliver is every recruiter's idea
of a poster subject, but surrounded as he is by a dozen
TAC IPs who are all combat-experienced, he exhibits ad-
mirable modesty that the older heads admire—but not to
his face. Cliver is part of B Flight of the 26th Cobra
Squadron, a flight made up of Captain John Schoeppner,
an experienced pilot transferred from another command,
First Lieutenant Henry Sherard—who graduated from
Moody AFB with Cliver out of Class 66-G—Cliver himself,
and led by an RAF exchange pilot, Squadron Leader Jock
Heron, a Scot with experienced hands and a tart tongue.

It was barely dawn when Cliver stood before his maps
in the six-by-nine briefing room in Cobra Operations.
Cliver was delivering the fruits of a long night's labor over
a mission folder. Cliver, acting as flight leader, had been
ordered to lay on an armed recce-ground-attack mission
against an airfield and a SAM site. Cliver had the chart
and knew the distances and headings, but had to figure out
routes and airspeeds and altitudes and takeoff weights and
time-over-target and how to reach the point where we
would simulate rendezvous with the tankers at a specified
time and which course and altitudes to fly to avoid flak

and how best to deal with the possibility of a MIG attack —everything, all the variables and temperatures at takeoff and pressure altitude over the target and fuel consumption at preferred airspeeds, in order to strike at the SAMs with rockets and bombs at precisely 10:10 hours and get us home again to land at 10:40 hours.

Cliver's neatly executed map was marked in bold black lines where the MIGs were, the tanker rendezvous area, the Star of David, and the airfield. It was the same kind of map he and Hank Sherard and Johnny Schoeppner would be seeing a lot more of in the months to come. It was a map of the face of the enemy. Cliver's relaxed briefing lasted more than an hour, broken only by a few questions from the other pilots and some probing reminders by Jock Heron. There was time for one last cup of coffee, one last trip to the head, one final cigarette before climbing into G-suits, zipping everything up, picking up parachutes and helmet bags, and walking outside into the cold to find airplanes with the right tail numbers. There were whole ranks of F-105Ds, the older B models, and several of the two-seater F-105Fs. Heron and I walked toward one of the latter, camouflaged flat brown-and-green like all the rest, bearing the tail number 8337. You mount a Thud like climbing up the side of a house, hand over hand up a vertical ladder, passing just in front of the wicked-looking left airscoop and then into the cockpit, right boot on the flat seat, left boot off the ladder, hands on the canopy rails, right boot down on the deck on the opposite side of the stick, then plopping down hard on what is surely the hardest seat of any airplane yet designed. The seat is the top part of the survival kit —a necessary item if you have to punch out over the wilds of the Nevada desert-mountain country.

One, two, three, and four the engines are started, their roar echoing off the little sugarloaf mountain that runs parallel to the main Nellis runway. Cliver and his wingman get off first in an element takeoff, climbing steeply away in AB, dragging pale-orange fire behind them. Three goes next, and when Heron lights off the burner to follow, you feel the kick in the back from the sudden acceleration and stay pressed against the chute pack. We quickly reach and pass our refusal speed of 172 knots, and at 186 knots the big Thud gets its wheels off the ground with 4800 feet of runway behind us. The world falls away, and we are climbing. Heron comes out of burner; I go forward against the straps and begin looking around. It's just like they said: riding the back of an F is like being inside a Link with side panels—you can't see a damn thing forward. The F-105F, in fact, cannot be landed from the rear cockpit. However, the view out either side of the canopy is unobstructed, giving a good sweep of the tops of the rugged hills below which we fly en route to the target. After a while Cliver leads us above the tops and we are quite high—at least five thousand feet above ground level. Flying Number Four position gives you an excellent view of a tactical formation, spread far apart, and the individual airplanes, big as they are, in war paint are very difficult to separate from the terrain below, even when you know where to look. This camouflage paint job added nearly 300 pounds to the weight of each F-105, but pilots say the weight penalty is worth the small cost in performance. Nothing, they say, sticks out so clearly over the jungles of North Vietnam as a silver airplane glinting in the sun.

One of the F-105s begins to slide nearer, then drifts

slowly across the top of the canopy and keeps on sliding
across the sky to take up position two thousand feet off
our starboard wing. "He shouldn't be there," Heron observed. "I'll just watch a bit and see how long it takes
him to realize he belongs off our other wing." Sure
enough, four minutes later the errant Thud quickly left
the new, and wrong, slot and moved smartly back
through the formation to take up position to our port.

We made it to the tanker rendezvous area well within
the time margin allowed, then turned sharply 90 degrees
and dropped down into a flatland, a shallow, barren valley stretching away between low hills splotched softly
with patches of new snow. We were running in toward
the target some miles away across a gentle mountain
range. Cliver led the flight in a shifting, weaving pattern
so that the two-ship elements were constantly scissoring
across the valley in a series of mild, level S-turns. We
rushed across the stark terrain at 500 knots, less than
600 feet above the ground. At this low altitude, speed
has very real meaning and you can sense the delicacy
with which Heron moves the stick. The mountain rushes
at us. On the other side, the target. Now the flight ceases
to weave. Cliver honks back on the stick, followed by the
other pilots. We climb very fast, clearing the top of the
rocky prominence in the pop-up maneuver calculated to
gain complete surprise over the enemy below. As the
mountain falls away, disappears, the SAM site comes
sharply into view. Then it, too, fades as Heron keeps up
the G in a climb that will afford him a grandstand view
of his students going in low to unload ordnance.

One of the 105s peels out of its climb and banks into a
steep, descending turn. His wings come level and he races

for the sandbagged communication/command post located dead center in the Star of David. We see the raked wings of the attacker flash across the desert, then a bright-red cherry mushroom in a cloud of white smoke. The strike is left and long. Number Two comes in and his practice bomb is long, but centered. Then Three makes his pass, and his bomb misses the site altogether. Because the plane doing the bombing is already past the target at the time of the strike, others call the strike for him after each run. We, who are orbiting the target from directly above, can see the strikes better than the others, and Heron calls the shots as they fall.

On the second pass over the SAMs the F-105s streak in on different headings, coming in from all directions of the clock. Number One, who made his first pass boring in from 7 o'clock, turns hard and comes in at 12 o'clock. Two, who came in at 8 o'clock, now strikes along the 1 o'clock axis, and Three comes in at 4 after his first pass from 9 o'clock. Thus the target is criss-crossed from all directions, and pilots must fly with their heads up and their eyes open. They are barely 300 feet off the deck, going like hell, trying to keep the pipper on the sight where it should be and flying so as to maintain a constant dive angle of 15 degrees before pull-out. They've got the corrections taped on this second pass. The telltale flashes of the 25 pounds of high explosive are dotted very near the center of the command post, and Cliver's bomb plunges directly into the sandbags. Heron, who is the IP, does not drop. There is such a shortage in this country of even practice bombs that all must be saved for students. No IPs are allowed to expend ordnance on training missions, which can only mean that the IPs, who never get a chance to practice, over a period of

Approach, pop-up, roll in and press the button to deliver sudden death.

time will lose their hard edge of proficiency while that of their students continues to improve.

It is from the ground, watching the 105s roll in to attack, that you can sense the terror enemy infantry and flak gunners must feel when a flight of Thuds pops up seemingly from nowhere and dives down to unload select ordnance. Qualification in gunnery at Nellis is done at one of the controlled ranges, where the range officer and his assistants monitor the strikes from towers, using binoculars to spot the distance the practice bombs strike from the center of the target, an orange tetrahedron inside a 300-foot-diameter circle.

The 105s, spaced fifteen seconds apart, roll in from 12,000 feet, seen from below as bullet shapes with tiny, thin wings. They flash in in 45-degree dives, doing 450 knots, and reach the "pickle point" one mile from target 5000 feet above the earth. They come out of the dive with a 4G pull-up and thunder overhead, climbing away. You can sometimes see the BDU-33 practice bombs—which have the same trajectory as live 750-pound high-explosive bombs—as a slender, dark blur as they leave the bomb-dispenser slung underneath the fuselage and arc toward the tetrahedron. I have seen strikes as close as sixteen feet from the target center, which is good bombing for any student.

The 2.75-inch FFAR (Folding Fin Aerial Rocket) rockets are used against the same chipped, battered tetrahedrons, but are released at much lower altitudes, closer to the target, and while the aircraft is in a shallower dive. The 105s roll in and level out to fire 2500 feet above ground level at a slant range of 4700 feet from target center. The bird is nosed down 30 degrees when the rockets are loosed, then pulled up steeply to avoid ground fire. First there is the rolling thunder of the J75 engine, then a loud *crack* as the rocket is fired and goes supersonic a split second later, then the crash of the explosion as the warhead makes contact with the ground. Then the tower shakes as the Thud pulls up and away.

It is the nose-mounted 20-mm. "Gatling gun," however, that provides the 105 with its deadliest accuracy in a ground support role. This gun is a six-barreled affair carrying 1014 rounds of high-explosive incendiary ammunition. The barrels rotate at a fantastic clip, firing at a rate of 6000 rounds per minute. At a range of 1000 feet, a Gatling gun properly harmonized will put a half-second burst of 49 rounds in a group tight enough to encircle with two hooped arms. The pilots fire at black bulls painted high on white targets twenty feet square. They set the mode switch on downwind leg, then set the master armament switch to ON on base leg, just prior to turn on final. They come in fast, at 500 knots, and shallow for maximum accuracy. At a 15-degree dive angle the pilot puts the pipper square on the bull. He must fly with absolute precision. The ball on the turn-and-slip indicator must be centered or the bullet strike will be a line error in the direction the ball has assumed. If he is pulling positive Gs, he will undershoot; if he has the airplane in a negative G situation, he will overshoot. He must get everything lined up and press the red button on the stick before reaching the foul line, 1600 feet from the target panels. If not, his high Mach will run him into danger of low pull-out, overstressing the airplane, flying into his own ricochets, or even mushing into the desert floor with fatal consequences. Any pilot who fouls on a strafing run is sent home for the rest of the day, whether he has completed his bombing and strafing runs

or not. The sound of an airborne Gatling is like the sound of no other gunfire: a brief, brutal ripping of heavy canvas. If a pilot ever gets his pipper square on target—an enemy truck convoy, MIG, flak gun—that target is a goner.

Watching these strikes from the ground, as the Vietcong see them, reveals another side of the coin as well, i.e., what guts it takes for a pilot to fly into the face of heavy ground fire at altitudes low enough to provide maximum accuracy. There is a long moment when the Thud, fast as it is, is committed to its firing pass and is flying along a constant path. You can track them with your naked eye and see how easy it is to follow their trajectory while they are "wired" to the target. You can imagine how easy no-deflection shots are when equipped with radar-laid 85-mm. guns (manu-factured and provided by the Russians) and smaller auto-matic weapons (made and given by both the Russians and the Chinese) and even rifles and pistols (which come mostly from the Chinese). One twenty-cent rifle ball, prop-erly placed in the vulnerable innards of a 105, can bring down a two-million-dollar airplane and its irreplaceable pilot. But the pilots keep coming—just as they did over Schweinfurt more than twenty years ago—and to get bombs on target they will come in lower, higher, straighter—or whatever may be necessary to carry out the assigned mis-sion.

To help Tactical Air Command with what accountants and other chairborne types refer to as "cost effectiveness," i.e., the maximum amount of damage inflicted upon the enemy at least cost in lives and airplanes, there is direct liaison between the unique Fighter Weapons School and combat squadrons operating out of Vietnam and Thailand. The Fighter Weapons School is both a gunnery training ground for USAF's fighter-pilot elite and a laboratory for combat techniques.

The Fighter Weapons School is part of the Center, but is separate from the Combat Crew Training Wings at Nellis and at other TAC training bases. The mission of the school is to update and polish select volunteers from TAC bases worldwide in latest weapons techniques that evolve from combat situations in Vietnam and are developed within the school itself at Nellis. The course runs for thirteen weeks, broken down into fifty-four training days, thirty-five sorties totaling thirty-nine hours, and a killing schedule of nearly two hundred and twenty hours of technical academics dealing with all phases of weapons delivery. The Fighter Weapons School handles student gunnery instructors on F-4D Phantom IIs, F-100D Supersabres and modified F-105s equipped with a new—and secret—radar system. The people who fly these classified Thuds call themselves The Wild Weasels, and the work they are doing in the Nevada desert will contribute endless woe and unpleasant surprises for "Charles Baby" in North Vietnam.

To qualify for the IP course in the Fighter Weapons School a pilot must have 1500 hours of flying time, including a minimum of 500 hours in the particular aircraft he is currently flying on operations. Graduates are sent back to their original units with a new diploma and a fund of weaponry knowledge which they pass on to the pilots in their squadron. It is a course for specialists, and the classes are small. The F-4 students, for instance, never number more than eight at one time; only twenty-four are graduated each year. It's a tough course and requires tough men to pass. Academics begin at 0600, followed by lengthy, detailed briefing for the first mission of the day. An hour

Lethal mating: Danny Wright and F-4C Phantom.

In a sun-splashed mirror, seeking a supersonic enemy.

of hard flying is followed by debriefing, which in turn is followed by more academics, followed by another briefing, a second mission, and so on until the pilot finds that he is suddenly tired and that the sun has gone down on a full day—and there are still four hours of study ahead after dinner. The temptation, under such unrelenting pressure, is strong to head for the pleasures of Las Vegas on Saturday night and hold forth on the Strip until the small hours. However, there is always an informal review held each Sunday for pilots of the Weapons School, and Saturday's bon vivant is generally Sunday's class dunce. The men of the FWS squadrons are tough, mature, and proud. All of the IPs have completed at least one tour of combat duty in Southeast Asia and, like the instructors at the 26th Cobras down the line, know what they are talking about.

One of these men, who wears the Outstanding Graduate patch on his shoulder, is Captain Christopher Daniel Wright, who has been flying USAF fighters since 1954. Wright, who is built like a pro football quarterback, spent 236 hours in aerial combat in Asia. One mission lasted seven long hours. Wright's F-4C delivered its ordnance on a target far inside North Vietnam, then on the way home was refueled and called in on a RESCAP mission for a downed flyer, was refueled again in the air, then was called in on a second RESCAP job. Refueled once again, Wright was allowed to fly back home.

Danny Wright, a man obviously and justifiably proud of the work the Fighter Weapons School is doing, explained that one of the more challenging assignments he and others like him face is finding solutions to problems encountered during combat operations in Vietnam. "Let's suppose," Wright said, "that the war situation one day requires our pilots to strike at enemy airfields in the North. We know that there is a steady buildup of Russian MIGs going on. The latest models. All-weather interceptors. Our recce photographs have given us exact details of how the VC protect these fighters while parked on their airstrips. They place them inside revetments twenty feet high, covered with camouflage mesh. The revetments are usually made of heavy sandbags, which are resistant to blast effects. One solution might be to saturate the entire airfield from high altitude with 750-pound bombs. But this kind of saturation bombing would probably mean a few overs or unders, causing civilian casualties. We're after the MIGs, not personnel. We could go in low, trying to place individual seven-fifties inside the revetment openings, but a near miss is no good; all you do is blow dirt. Then again, the openings probably face in different directions, meaning repeated run-ins on each revetment—and that means long exposure to ground fire. Same objection applies to ordinary napalm bombs, which tumble.

"What we did was this. We built an exact replica of a VC revetment for MIGs on one of the uncontrolled ranges right here at Nellis. We ran a lot of math studies on the problem, studying it from all angles. Then we went out in F-4s and put the theoretical solutions to the test. What we finally arrived at as a solution was the use of finned napalm, delivered by dive bombing at an angle of 28.5 degrees. We work out solutions to tactical problems of this nature constantly here. Conversely, TAC out in the combat zone sends us solutions to problems they have found effective over there. These workable procedures are put straight into the syllabus and are passed on to the Combat Crew Training Wings. Thus pilots graduating

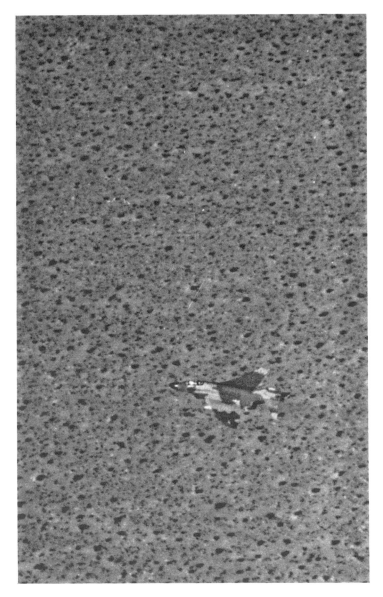

Camouflage.

from squadrons like the 26th are kept current when they get orders to join their new outfits in SEA."

Strapping yourself to an F-4D is more complicated than hooking up inside a T-38 or an F-105. You walk away from the locker room wearing G-suit and carrying a helmet, but instead of having to lug a heavy parachute out to the flight line you wear only a lightweight web harness. Phantoms use the British Martin-Baker ejection seats with the chute an integral part of the seat. An aircrewman hooks your harness to the chute, then hooks up the shoulder straps. You plug in the G-suit and oxygen connections, but he helps you with a pair of heavy web leg restrainers which will keep your legs from flopping in case you punch out. Just over your head are a pair of striped hand grips which, when pulled, lower a protective face curtain and initiate the entire ejection sequence. "Let's not bother with that," Danny Wright said. "That's not an Air Force method. Navy guys use it. Go for the secondary release next to the edge of the seat, between your legs. Grab it with both hands and pull. The first four inches blows the canopy, another four inches of travel and you go out."

We taxied behind four other hot-breathing F-4s toward the armament area, a wide place just before you turn off to enter the active runway, where crewmen duck underneath the wings to pull the remaining red-streamered safety pins that make the ordnance live. The four Phantoms going after a SAM site and open POL (petroleum-oil-lubricant) stores were loaded with a little of everything in the inventory, but Three and Four carried only Mk. 82 Snakeye bombs. These are high-explosive bombs with folding fins. When the bomb is released, a shaft slides out of the rear of the casing and four heavy metal fins deploy,

acting like a drogue chute. This gives the pilot who makes his run at low altitude time to get out of the way of the blast.

"On this mission," Captain Wright explained, "we're going to be the Bad Guys. The Good Guys are in the other F-4s, and we're going to see if we can bounce them en route to the target and maybe mix it up a little. The other pilots were briefed that we might jump them, but they don't know when or where. It's good practice. Makes everybody stay sharp, keep their eyes peeled."

Although an F-4 weighs nearly as much as the heavy Thud, the Phantom is a twin-engined airplane with much lower wing loading. Thus when we got into burner on takeoff the kick in the rump was more substantial and we lifted off sooner. The two right-hand drums on the calibrated airspeed dial spun in a white blur, too fast to read. We got off the runway behind the Good Guys and hung in there in loose formation. A few minutes later, Wright pulled us away to starboard to begin the serious game of hide-and-seek. We chased over the gashed brown ridges fifty or sixty feet over the ground doing 450 knots, and we kept that speed. Wright kept the F-4 low, hidden on one side of a range of low hills guarding a valley, then he came back on the stick and we popped up over the crests, turned hard right, and entered the dry valley.

"See them?" Wright asked. I did, with difficulty. The Good Guys were spread wide in tactical formation, their mottled skins difficult to separate from the earth below. We were higher than the other F-4s, and Wright began closing in. Anxiously we watched the other airplanes grow larger. They held rigid, perfect formation. It looked as though Wright was going to achieve a perfect surprise.

Then, laconically: "Bogie. Six o'clock high." One of the Good Guys had spotted us. There would be no bounce. But Wright pressed on and began to close with Four, who began to rack it around in a tight turn. Wright followed, and the Gs began to build. The accelerometer needle flipped to 4.5 and stayed there. The hard turn lasted for what seemed long, brutal minutes. Drops of ice-cold sweat popped out from underneath the foam padding on my helmet and pattered onto my gloves and boots. Wright held the turn. "How are you back there?"

"No sweat," I answered, which wasn't strictly true. The G-suit was doing its work, squeezing my abdomen and legs hard, and I was nowhere near blackout. But tunnel vision is a definite handicap when you desperately want to take advantage of the excellent vision offered by the F-4's canopy. I could not see the Good Guy ahead of us, or the Good Guy who had tacked on our tail. Finally the mock combat was broken off and we honked up to follow the other F-4s to the target.

"In combat we often pull six or seven Gs," Wright explained. "You really have to reef it in, to out-turn and out-G the other guy. Constant practice gives fighter pilots a fairly strong set of neck muscles." I believed him.

We orbited overhead as the other Phantoms roared in low over the target, clobbering the SAMs and the petroleum-oil-lubricant stores. The F-4s splattered the desert floor with their ordnance. Wright called the strikes; then we went off to practice acro.

Somehow, the others thought we were still playing the part of the Bad Guy. Wright split-essed the F-4, executed a flawless Immelmann, and was at the top of a very high loop when our earphones crackled with a voice calling

excitedly. "High! High! High!" Wright said later he thought it was some sort of greeting. But it was a Good Guy who had spotted us far overhead, believing Wright was ready to pounce. The F-4s below braced to meet the attack. They watched in puzzlement as Wright completed one loop, then entered another, followed by a series of low-G S-turns. Everybody relaxed and we closed up in tight formation and raced for home.

In five-second intervals the F-4s peeled off and entered the Nellis traffic pattern. One instant the Phantom riding four feet off our left wingtip was there, very large, then all we saw was his light-colored belly and wings flipping away, falling off, growing smaller. ". . . thousand and four, one thousand and five." Wright banked the big fighter over, and we followed the others onto the downwind leg. We flared out and touched down at a slow, stable 110 knots, popped the chute, and rolled smoothly down the long strip and turned off the runway.

Pilots in other F-4s waved.

Down there, everybody is Good Guys.

Appendix A

UNDERGRADUATE PILOT TRAINING SCHEDULE

Flying Training	Flying Hours	Total Hours [1]
Policies & Procedures, T-41		5:00
Contact, T-41	30:00	60:00
Policies & Procedures, T-37		12:45
Contact, T-37	55:40	111:20
Instrument, T-37	22:40	45:20
Navigation, T-37	7:40	15:20
Formation, T-37	4:00	8:00
Link Trainer, T-37		22:30
Policies & Procedures, T-38		28:00
Contact, T-38	35:00	70:00
Instrument, T-38	29:30	59:00
Navigation, T-38	18:20	36:40
Formation, T-38	34:00	68:00
Link Trainer, T-38		32:30
Optional Training	3:20	6:40
TOTAL	240:10	573:05

[1] Includes classroom and flight line briefing time.

Academic Training	Total Hours
Airmanship	17:00
Aviation Physiology, T-37	28:00
Physiological Support	10:00
Aircraft Engineering, T-37	19:00
Instrument Proc. & Radio Aids	14:00
Principles of Flight	10:00
Flight Instruments	13:00
Aural & Visual Code	8:00
Navigation	25:00
Flying Safety	6:00
Flight Planning, T-37	37:00
Weather	44:00
Aviation Physiology, T-38	4:00
Aircraft Engineering, T-38	19:00
Instrument Proc. & Radio Aids, T-38	16:00
Flight Planning, T-38	35:00
Applied Aerodynamics	28:00
Reciprocating Engines	11:00
Radar	5:00
TOTAL	349:00

Officer Training	Total Hours
Orientation & Processing	28:00
Heritage	17:00
Duty	22:00
Counterinsurgency	11:00
Drill, Ceremonies, Inspections	24:00
Physical Development	125:00
Marksmanship	10:00
TOTAL	237:00

Appendix B

GLOSSARY OF EVERYDAY TERMS

A

AB: Afterburner.

ABORT: To discontinue, cancel, or halt. Usually used in association with takeoffs that cannot be completed because of difficulty with engines or hydraulic systems.

ADC: Air Defense Command.

AFFIRMATIVE: Yes.

ALTIMETER SETTING: A pressure reading set into the altimeter to adjust for the existing barometic pressure. Standard pressure at sea level is expressed as 29.92 (in inches of mercury). The pressure reading is set into a cut-out in the face of the altimeter known as the Kollsman window.

ALTITUDE, ABSOLUTE: The altitude of an aircraft above the surface or terrain over which it is flying.

ALTITUDE, INDICATED: That altitude read from the altimeter.

ALTITUDE, PRESSURE: The altitude read from the altimeter when the Kollsman window is set at 29.92.

ALTITUDE, DENSITY: Pressure altitude corrected for temperature.

ALTITUDE, TRUE: The true height of the aircraft above sea level.

ANTICOLLISION LIGHTS: High-intensity rotating red beacons mounted on most aircraft, which are designed to prevent midair collisions.

ATTITUDE: The position of the aircraft in relation to a fixed reference, usually the horizon.

APU: Auxiliary power unit. An external power source used for ground starts of jet engines. Also known as JASU, jet aircraft starting unit.

AROUND THE HORN: Movement of the throttle from OFF to IDLE, or the reverse.

B

BACK PRESSURE: Pressure applied to the control stick which raises the elevator surfaces, thus increasing pitch attitude.

BALLOON: To float upward from the runway when attempting to land as a result of applying too much back pressure in relation to the airspeed.

BARRIER: Arresting device placed at very end of runway to snare aircraft that have landed too long or too hot, or whose brakes have failed.

BEHIND THE POWER CURVE: A condition of flight in which the thrust required is greater than the thrust available.

BELLY IN: To land an aircraft with the gear still in the wells. Not recommended for T-37s, T-38s, or any of the Century fighters.

BEND IT AROUND: Slang for "fly the aircraft more aggressively." Also, RACK IT AROUND, REEF IT IN.

BLACKOUT: Temporary loss of vision or consciousness caused by a fall of blood pressure in the head with resultant insufficiency of oxygen. Caused by pulling excessive positive Gs.

BLAST PAD: Specified location on the runway or apron for run-up of jet engines. Constructed specifically to withstand high-temperature backwash from the tailpipe.

BLIP: Radar return.

BLURP: Noise made when jet engine switches from one fuel control system to another.

BOGIE: Any flying aircraft that the pilot can see, or radar operator can see as a scope return or blip. Bogies are not necessarily assumed to be unfriendly aircraft.

BOOM BUCKET: The MA-15 ejection-seat trainer.

BOONDOCKS: To Marines, a wild uninhabited area. To pilots, any field, meadow, or pasture, as opposed to a standard runway.

BREAK: Hard bank, port or starboard. Used in air-to-air combat to warn another pilot to turn away from an enemy on his tail.

BREAK OUT: Term used to clear one or all aircraft from a traffic pattern or formation.

BROKEN UP: Radio transmission that has been interfered with intermittently.

BUFFETING: Knocking about sustained by an aircraft surface when turbulence or stall is encountered.

BURBLE: Separation in the boundary layer of air surrounding a streamlined body which results in divergent velocities and pressures, especially over the upper surface of an airfoil. Burble causes loss of lift and increased drag.

C

CALL INITIAL (TO): Identification call by pilot to mobile controller when aircraft is turning on initial approach for landing.

CAS: Calibrated air speed. The indicated airspeed corrected for installation error, i.e., the difference between the differential pressure established by the Pitot tube and the theoretical pressure that should be developed.

CEILING: Maximum height at which an aircraft can fly. In weather, an overcast of clouds above a given area limiting visibility.

CENTURY SERIES FIGHTERS: USAF Tactical aircraft, including the F-100, F-101, F-102, F-104, F-105, and F-106.

CHOCK TIME: That time designated for any group of aircraft to be parked on the apron.

CHOP: To reduce throttle rapidly to idle.

CLOSED TRAFFIC: A specific type of aircraft traffic pattern normally used in emergencies for jet aircraft. This type of pattern enables a pilot to position his aircraft for landing in the shortest possible time with the least amount of fuel from a go-around.

COBBED: Throttle full open.

COCKED NOSEWHEEL: Nosewheel that has swiveled beyond controllable limits.

CONTACT FLYING: Flight in which the pilot determines attitude and position by visual reference to clouds and landmarks on the earth. The oldest kind of flying known to man.

CONTRAIL: Condensation vapor caused by hot exhaust gases condensing moisture in cold air. Contrails are usually formed at altitudes from 30,000 to 45,000 feet at air temperatures ranging from −50 to −65 degrees F.

CRAB: To turn an aircraft partly into the wind to compensate for drift.

CRITICAL MACH NUMBER: Speed beyond which an aircraft is not stressed for safe flight; indicated by red marker on Machmeter.

CROSS CONTROL: Uncoordinated (opposed) use of aircraft controls.

CRUISING LEVEL FLIGHT: Operating the aircraft in level flight with normal power settings.

D

DF: Direction finding.

DISH OUT: Flight path resulting from improper use of controls, characterized by nosing down and to the side.

DNIF: Duty not including flying.

DRAG CHUTE: Small nylon parachute stowed at tail of aircraft for release by pilot during landing roll to reduce ground speed.

DRAGGED IN: A long, low approach to the runway using power.

D-RING: Alloy D-shaped ring that is pulled to deploy a parachute canopy. The D-ring is located on the left side of the chest, just below armpit level.

DROP IN: To stall an aircraft while landing high enough above ground so that it slams hard against the runway.

E

EAC: Expected approach clearance.

EAR DEFENDERS: Plastic and foam cups placed over ears of pilots and ground crew to protect sensitive eardrums from damage caused by jet engine sounds. Also known as BUNNY EARS, these devices are musts for anyone working around T-37s.

ECHELON: Placement of aircraft in stairstepped angular line of formation. Also, level of command.

EGT: Exhaust gas temperature.

EXTERNAL STORES: Bombs, napalm, rockets, or nuclear devices mounted on special racks underneath wings.

F

FLAK: From the German *flieger-abwehrkanone,* antiaircraft cannon. More especially, the hot metal shards fired from exploding shells by radar-laid, Russian-manufactured 90-mm. guns, which have caused such heavy losses of American aircraft by ground fire in Vietnam.

FLAMEOUT: Sudden loss of fire in a jet engine with consequent loss of power.

FLAP: To get into a highly agitated state, such as sustaining flameout while trying to become airborne. Base commanders are occasionally subject to flaps upon sudden, unexpected appearance of the AIG, the Air Inspector General.

FLIGHT LEVEL (FL): An altitude designation that has superseded the familiar "angels" term. An attitude of 29,000 feet would be written as FL 290.

FOD: Foreign object damage. Powerful suction from jet engine intakes can suck in nuts, bolts, screwdrivers, and other objects which are ingested into engines, causing extensive damage.

FULL DRAG: Condition in which gear, flaps, and speed brake are extended.

FULL STOP: Landing followed by turn off at taxiway.

G

GCA: Ground-controlled approach. A radar-assisted approach to a runway in conditions of poor or no visibility.

GARBAGE: Extended devices that result in increased, unwanted drag, such as gear, flaps, and speed brakes. On takeoff, you get all the garbage up as soon as possible.

GO AROUND: To continue in the traffic pattern without or instead of landing. Known as a wave-off to Navy pilots.

GOLDEN KEY: The parachute arming lanyard anchor, a solid brass ring attached to the swivel link on M-5 and M-6 seat belts. In case of ejection, the golden key ensures that the automatic opening of the parachute after seat separation will begin. The sequencing can also be manually initiated by tugging a round, orange wooden ball.

GREASE IN: To make an exceptionally smooth landing.

GREEN APPLE: The round wooden knob that activates the bail-out oxygen bottle.

GIVE IT THE NEEDLE: Use maximum power available.

GROUND TRACK: The path over the earth an aircraft describes while in flight.

H

HEAD UP AND LOCKED: Term instructors often use when referring to student manifesting inattention.

HOLD IT OFF: To hold the aircraft off the ground until proper landing attitude has been established.

HOME IN ON: To fly toward a ground radio navigational aid using the plane's own radio navigational equipment.

HOOD: A visor used to block out outside references when practicing instrument flying.

HOT START: Excessive EGT after start of jet engine. Often results in severe damage.

HOT MIKE: Interphone system that permits pilot and instructor to communicate without use of microphone switches.

I

IAS: Indicated airspeed.

IFR: Instrument flight rules, as opposed to VFR.

INITIAL APPROACH: Approach of an aircraft preparatory to beginning a landing procedure.

INTERPHONE: Any telephone, microphone, or receiver by which aircrew or instructor and student communicate with each other. Admonitions given by the IP to student who has head up and locked cannot be heard by mobile control or others, who receive on separate channels.

IN THE GREEN: Specifically, engine instruments indicating that engines are operating within prescribed limitations.

IP: Instructor pilot.

J

JASU: Jet aircraft starting unit. See APU.

JET STREAM: High-velocity winds at altitude whose speeds vary from 50 to 200 knots. Pilots can often plan flights to ride these variable winds to their advantage.

JET WASH: Exhaust that emerges from a jet tailpipe. Must be watched when flying in-trail formation or when taking off or landing behind other aircraft, because of turbulence involved.

JP-4: Jet propellant four, a kerosene-based fuel used to power military jet aircraft.

K

KNOT: One nautical mile per hour, or 6,080.20 feet.

L

LABS: Low altitude bombing system. Method used by TAC pilots, to deliver nuclear bombs on target, that allows flight away from impending holocaust without harm; a form of toss bombing that sees the nuclear device headed one way, the aircraft another.

LETDOWN AREA: Area designated for aircraft to make descents from cruising altitude preparatory to approach and landing.

LOCAL AREA: Prescribed airspace limits for an air base out of which students may not fly without prior clearance.

M

MACH: Speed of a moving body relative to the speed of sound in the medium through which it moves. Mach 1 at sea level is approximately 760 mph. At higher, colder altitudes the speed of sound is less—about 660 mph at 35,000 feet.

MANIFOLD PRESSURE: Pressure in the intake manifold of an internal combustion engine; expressed in inches of mercury.

MAYDAY: International radio distress call, from the French *m'aidez.*

MINIMUM FUEL: That fuel which is held in reserve for emergencies.

MOBILE CONTROL: Small control tower located near runway.

MUSH: To gain little or no altitude, or to lose altitude when the pitch angle would normally indicate a gain. When referring to aircraft controls *per se,* mushy describes the reaction precisely.

N

NEGATIVE: No; permission denied.

NUKE: Abbreviation for nuclear weapon.

O

OUT AND BACK: Cross-country flight that involves landing at another base, refueling, and returning home the same day.

OVERRUN: That portion of a runway at either end which has not been properly prepared for takeoff or landing. Some overruns have been graded and surfaced, but others have been merely cleared of obstacles so that a miscalculation in landing will result in minimum damage to aircraft.

P

PAINT: To receive a radar return on the scope.

PENETRATION: Instrument letdown from an intermediate altitude; flight through a thunderstorm.

PINK SLIP: Failing grade.

PINS: Metal clips or pins used to prevent some system of the aircraft from being used. Down-lock pins are placed in the landing gear of all aircraft while parked on the ground to prevent inadvertent retraction. Pins are used in all ejection systems to prevent ground firing of canopy and seat.

PITCHOUT: Making a steep turn from straight line of flight to enter the landing pattern.

PORPOISE: Cycle of violent bouncing from nose gear to main gear after touchdown on runway. Usually caused by trying to force aircraft on runway nosewheel first.

PRANG: To crash; term borrowed from the RAF during World War II.

PRICE CHECK: Abbreviated reminder, or check list, used by USAF pilots to check oxygen equipment before flight. P = pressure; R = regulator; I = indicator; C = connections; E = emergency system.

PUZZLE PALACE: The Pentagon.

R

RAMP OUT: Radio call to announce that the aircraft has returned to parking place on ramp.

READ: To hear or understand clearly.

REDLINE: Red mark on airspeed indicator which shows safe maximum speed of aircraft, beyond which structural damage may be incurred. Redlines are used on other performance gauges to reveal danger points.

REDOUT: Temporary vision disturbance, sometimes accompanied by loss of consciousness, during which red haze films the eyes. Caused by pulling excessive negative Gs, which force too much blood to the head.

ROUNDOUT: To bring an aircraft down in a smooth flight path tangentially to the runway preparatory to touching down.

ROUND ROBIN: A cross-country flight in which takeoff and landing are made at the same field.

RSU: Runway supervisory unit; mobile control.

RUNWAY TRIM: One or more trim tabs operating out of control or remaining at a limit of travel as a result of electrical malfunction in the aircraft's trim mechanism.

RON: Remain overnight.

S

SAY AGAIN: Proper radio term for "Repeat your last transmission."

SECTION LINES: Ground boundaries between sections of land that can be used for maintaining orientation during certain kinds of aerobatics. Highways, roads, and fence lines serve as section lines for pilots who are trying to exit from a loop in the same direction from which it was entered.

SFO: Simulated flameout.

SHUTDOWN: Engine and related equipment turned off.

SIPHON: Fuel being lost overboard by suction or vacuum action.

SKIDDING: Sliding away from the center of a curve while turning. Rotation of the aircraft about the vertical axis when not accompanied by bank.

SKIN: Outside covering of an aircraft.

SKIN PAINT: Radar return from aircraft not using or not equipped with a transponder.

SLIP: Sliding toward the center of the curve while turning; occurs when the aircraft yaws and slides downward when the wings are banked.

STAGGER: Alignment of one aircraft to the side and to the rear of another aircraft. Takeoff or landing at specified time interval before or after other aircraft.

STANDBY ONE: Wait for further instructions or information.

STATIC PORT: Opening in an aircraft through which air is channeled to certain flight instruments that operate by static pressure. Static ports usually consist of needle-like holes unaffected by dynamic pressure.

STATUS OF FLYING: Specified types of flight missions currently permitted according to weather conditions.

STOPCOCK: Throttle off.

SURGE: Sudden, abnormal increase in power or energy.

T

TACAN: Tactical air navigation. A navigation radio hooked up to a needle that points to a selected station on the ground. TACAN is interconnected with the DME (Distance Measuring Equipment), which shows the distance in nautical miles from the aircraft to the particular ground station.

TAS: True airspeed. Equivalent airspeed corrected for air density error. Since density is a function of temperature, TAS is also in relation to temperature.

TOUCH AND GO: To land and take off in a continuous straight line without stopping.

U

UHF: Ultra high frequency.

UNDERSHOOT: To land—or crash—an aircraft short of the runway, or short of an intended line thereon.

UNREADABLE: Not understandable.

V

VALSALVA: Method of relieving pressure on eardrums during descent from altitude by closing mouth, pinching nostrils shut, and blowing gently, thus forcing air through the previously closed eustachian tube into the cavity of the middle ear and equalizing the pressure.

VHF: Very high frequency radio.

VOR: Abbreviation for VHF omnidirectional range. A radio compass effective in all directions and unaffected by storms and other atmospheric disturbances. The pilot flies a needle which keeps him on a preselected course.

W

WASHOUT: 1. A designed warp in an aircraft wing giving a decrease in the angle of attack toward the tip. 2. To fail a course or fall below minimum standards. 3. A totally destroyed aircraft.

WILCO: Radio term meaning "I will comply with your request."

WRITE UP: To report defects in an aircraft or discrepancies in flying techniques employed by personnel.

Z

ZERO LANYARD: The lanyard that is attached to the D-ring to provide instant, automatic deployment of the parachute in the event of ejection from a disabled aircraft.

ZILCH: Zero; nothing.

ZOOM AND BOOM: Technique employed when aircraft flames out or catches fire at low altitudes. Using available momentum, pilot increases pitch angle to maximum, trading airspeed for altitude, so that ejection from aircraft may be accomplished at maximum altitude.

Appendix C

PHOTOGRAPHY IN HIGH
PERFORMANCE AIRCRAFT

The decision as to which equipment to use for the air-to-air photographs for this book was based upon past experience while riding the rear cockpit of a T-33 some years ago with the 68th Fighter-Interceptor Squadron, and later as a guest of the USAF Thunderbirds when the solo man, Captain Gerald D. Larson, demonstrated what life can be like inside the cockpit of an F-100F. Space inside modern jet trainers and fighters is at an absolute premium. Mobility is restricted because of being strapped tightly, belly and shoulders, to the ejection seat. Framing through the viewfinder is made difficult by the protective obstructions of helmet, oxygen mask, and curved visor. Changing film must be accomplished while wearing long leather gloves, often during acrobatic and combat maneuvers. Under high-G loads the camera feels impossibly heavy. A 32-ounce camera and lens combination under 4 Gs, for example, weighs eight pounds. What you want, then, is the slimmest, lightest, least-complicated 35mm single-lens reflex camera available. Reflex viewing is important in order to avoid bothersome reflections from canopies, almost all of which are covered with hairline scratches that reflect sunlight in spectacular bursts. Reflex viewing also ensures precise framing; what your eye sees on the ground glass you get on the film.

The bulk of the air-to-air photographs were made with a single Honeywell Pentax H1-a 35mm single-lens reflex, which fulfills all requirements of lightness, reliability, and simplicity of operation for the job at hand. Lenses used while aloft were the 55mm f/2 and the 28mm f/3.5 Super-Takumars. This latter optic proved extremely useful in close-formation work because its 75-degree angle of coverage made it possible to squeeze in the entire length of such massive airplanes as the McDonnell F-4D Phantoms and the Republic F-105D Thunderchiefs riding only a few feet from our own aircraft. Because jets provide smooth, vibrationless flight, camera shake was never a problem. The same lenses were used on the ground, backed up by a 300mm f/5.6 Tele-Kilar. Also at hand was a 35mm auto-exposure camera manufactured by Minolta in Japan, but imported and modified by the General Aniline & Film Corporation in Binghamton, N.Y. This Autoset camera was modified for one-hand use by Mercury astronauts and is identical to the one used by Colonel John Glenn aboard Friendship 7 on this country's first orbital mission.

Film used throughout was either Ansco Versapan or Ansco Super-Hypan, both fast, fine-grained emulsions that lend themselves to "pushing" in development to achieve higher ASA indices and contrast modifications. Two great advantages of these films lie in the fact that the cartridges are very easy to open while in the darkroom, requiring no special tools or beer-can openers, and that each roll comes packed inside a light aluminum metal can, useful for storage and an aid for keeping temperature stabilized prior to development. The Versapan was exposed at ASA 320 and developed for 3¾ minutes in Acufine at a temperature of 70 degrees F. The Hypan was rated at ASA 1000 and developed in Acufine for 7 minutes at the same temperature. Exposures varied, but on an average were a consistent 1/500 second at f/11 aloft while shooting through a K2 (medium-yellow) filter with the Versapan.

No photographs were posed, and no special photo missions were laid on for the author's benefit.

Although the negatives were processed by the author, the final prints for this book were made by Modernage Photographic Services, Inc., in New York.

Diagrams of Characteristic
Flight Maneuvers

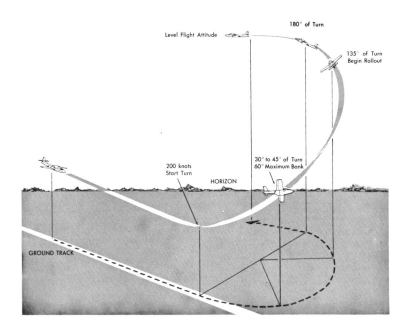

1. The Chandelle

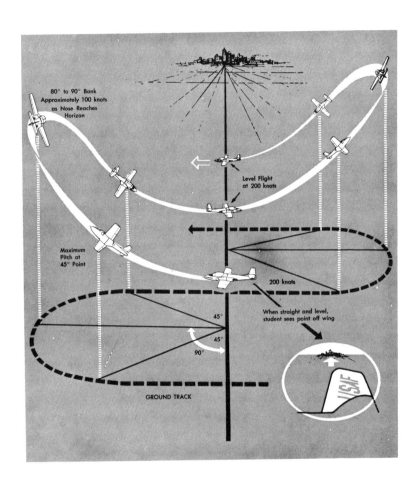

2. The Lazy Eight

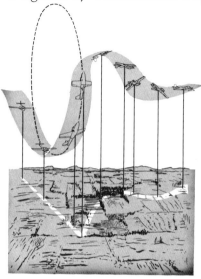

3. Vertical Recovery

4. The Barrel Roll

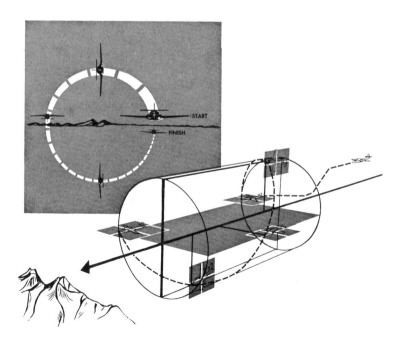

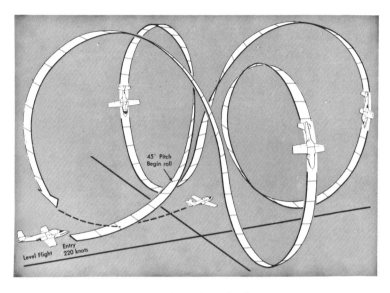

5. The Cloverleaf

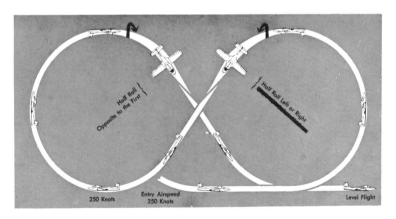

6. The Cuban Eight

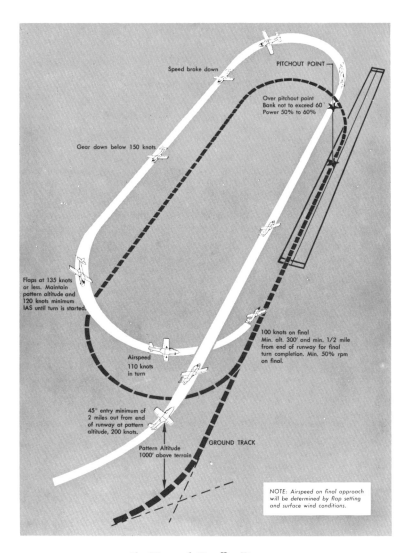

7. Normal Traffic Pattern

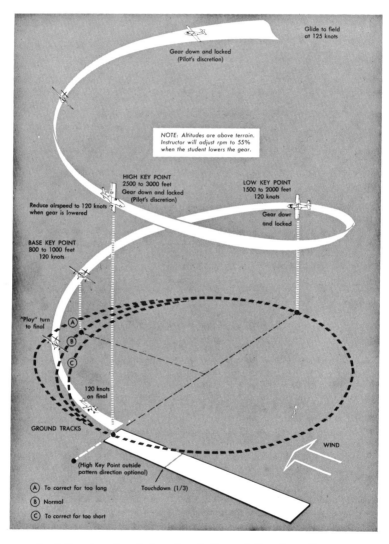

8. 360° Overhead Simulated Forced Landing Pattern

Index

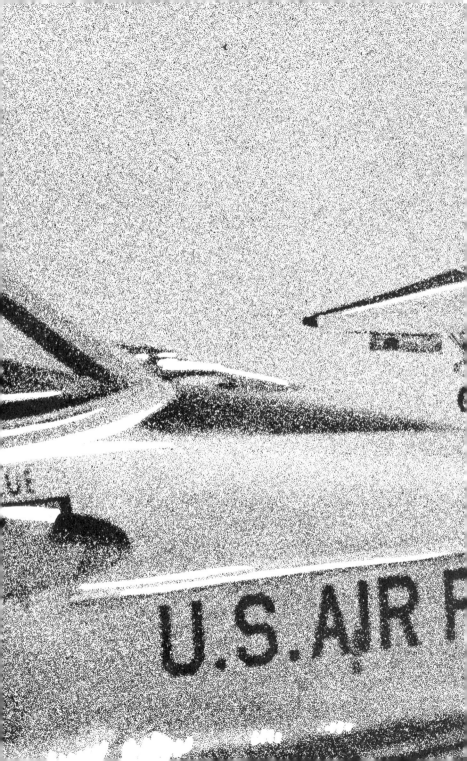